The Idea of the PhD

The Idea of the PhD: The doctorate in the twenty-first-century imagination analyses the PhD as it is articulated in diverse areas of contemporary discourse at a time in which the degree is undergoing growth, change and scrutiny worldwide. It considers not just institutional ideas of the PhD, but those of the broader cultural and social domain as well as asking whether, and to what extent, the idea of the Doctor of Philosophy, the highest achievable university award, is being reimagined in the twenty-first century.

In a world where the PhD is undergoing significant radical change, and where inside universities, doctoral enrolments are continually climbing, as the demand for more graduates with high-level research skills increases, this book asks the following questions:

- How do we understand how the PhD is currently imagined and conceptualised in the wider domain?
- Where will we find ideas about the PhD, from its purpose, to the nature of research work undertaken and the kinds of pedagogies engaged, to the researchers who undertake it and are shaped by it?

International in scope, this is a text that explores the culturally inflected representation of the doctorate and its graduates in the imagination, literature and media. *The Idea of the PhD* contributes to the research literature in the field of doctoral education and higher education. As such, it will be a fascinating text for researchers, postgraduates and academics interested in the idea of the university.

Frances Kelly is Senior Lecturer in the School of Critical Studies in Education, Faculty of Education and Social Work, University of Auckland, New Zealand

The Idea of the PhD

The doctorate in the twenty-first-century imagination

Frances Kelly

LONDON AND NEW YORK

First edition published 2017
by Routledge
2 Park Square, Milton Park, Abingdon, Oxon OX14 4RN

and by Routledge
711 Third Avenue, New York, NY 10017

Routledge is an imprint of the Taylor & Francis Group, an informa business

© 2017 Frances Kelly

The right of Frances Kelly to be identified as author of this work has been asserted by her in accordance with sections 77 and 78 of the Copyright, Designs and Patents Act 1988.

All rights reserved. No part of this book may be reprinted or reproduced or utilised in any form or by any electronic, mechanical, or other means, now known or hereafter invented, including photocopying and recording, or in any information storage or retrieval system, without permission in writing from the publishers.

Trademark notice: Product or corporate names may be trademarks or registered trademarks, and are used only for identification and explanation without intent to infringe.

British Library Cataloguing in Publication Data
A catalogue record for this book is available from the British Library

Library of Congress Cataloging-in-Publication Data
Names: Kelly, Frances, 1972-
Title: The idea of the PhD : the doctorate in the 21st century imagination / Frances Kelly.
Description: New York : Routledge, 2017.
Identifiers: LCCN 2016033826 (print) | LCCN 2016034830 (ebook) | ISBN 9781138900226 (hbk : alk. paper) | ISBN 9781138900233 (pbk : alk. paper) | ISBN 9781315707396 (ebk)
Subjects: LCSH: Doctor of philosophy degree.
Classification: LCC LB2386 .K46 2017 (print) | LCC LB2386 (ebook) | DDC 378.2—dc23
LC record available at https://lccn.loc.gov/2016033826

ISBN: 978-1-138-90022-6 (hbk)
ISBN: 978-1-138-90023-3 (pbk)
ISBN: 978-1-315-70739-6 (ebk)

Typeset in Minion
by Swales & Willis Ltd, Exeter, Devon, UK

Contents

	Acknowledgements	vii
	Introduction: the Doctor of Philosophy in the twenty-first-century imagination	1
1	**The nature of doctoral research**	13
2	**The idea of the PhD researcher**	41
3	**The idea of PhD pedagogy**	67
4	**The spaces of doctoral research**	91
	Concluding remarks: future imaginings	117
	References	121
	Index	132

Acknowledgements

Earlier versions of sections of chapters have been adapted from the following journal articles. I am grateful to the journal editors and to the reviewers for giving me the opportunity to develop, revise and publish this work, which has contributed greatly to the conceptualisation of this book.

A version of part of Chapter 3 appeared as:

F. Kelly (2009) 'Supervision satirised: fictional narratives of student–supervisor relationships', *Arts and Humanities in Higher Education* 8 (3): 368–384.

A version of part of Chapter 1 appeared as:

F. Kelly (2012) 'Seekers after truth? Images of postgraduate research and researchers in the twenty-first century', *Discourse: Studies in the Cultural Politics of Education* 33 (4): 517–528.

Parts of the following appear in Chapter 2:

F. Kelly (2013) 'And so betwixt them both: taking insights from literary analysis into higher education research', *Higher Education Research and Development* 32 (1): 70–82.

Thank you to the participants who took the time to share their ideas of the PhD. Colleagues whose conversations and company have challenged and encouraged me include academic staff and doctoral students in the School of Critical Studies in Education, in particular Cat Mitchell; the women of Tauhara; and colleagues in the fields of doctoral education and higher education at home and abroad. A special thanks to Barbara Grant, for the research fellowship (in both senses) and for being a true academic: people like you make the university.

My family, you are the centre of my life, especially Darren Sheehan and Finn Kelly-Sheehan, who tend the fires that warm me while I write.

Introduction
The Doctor of Philosophy in the twenty-first-century imagination

> ... in my opinion,
> Whoever wants to understand the truth of something
> Has to use his fantasy,
> Play with ideas, and find the key to the puzzle;
> And if you cannot reach it by the most direct route,
> There are a thousand other ways to help you.
> (Galileo, cited in Reynolds, 2002, p.55)

How do we understand how the PhD is currently imagined and conceptualised in the wider domain? Where will we find ideas about the PhD, from its purpose, to the nature of research work undertaken and the kinds of pedagogies engaged in, to the researchers who undertake it and are shaped by it? This book analyses the PhD as it is articulated in diverse areas of contemporary discourse at a time in which the degree is undergoing growth, change and scrutiny worldwide. It considers not just institutional ideas of the PhD but those of the broader cultural and social domain, and it asks whether, and to what extent, the idea of the Doctor of Philosophy, the highest achievable university award, is being reimagined in the twenty-first century.

As an extended critical analysis of the idea of the PhD in discourse, this book challenges the reader, who may be used to thinking in quite other terms, to consider the PhD *as* culturally determined and understood, and to recognise it as an idea formed in sites within *and* beyond the context of the university. By critiquing the PhD as it appears in novels, films and television series, as well as institutionally derived documents, we can gain insights into the meaning and importance it holds to society, and into those who undertake to attain a PhD degree. I could say, taking my cue from Gaston Bachelard (1994/1958) that this book offers an ontology of *images* of the PhD, or that, by examining cultural representations of the PhD alongside other texts, it undertakes a *poetics* of the PhD. Alternatively, I could say that I trace different stories that are told about the PhD: in popular culture; by individual PhD graduates and candidates; in institutional discourse; by governments and in the research literature in the early twenty-first century.

Are our ideas of the PhD very different from those of other historical contexts? Although it is not a historical study, this book considers the relationship between contemporary ideas of the PhD and those which we understand to have been in circulation during the degree's early beginnings. According to William Clark (2006), the Doctor of Philosophy has existed as an idea since the late eighteenth century. Although some give the decisive date of the first PhD as 1810, from the University of Berlin, Clark traces a more gradual emergence of the doctoral dissertation in the Germanic universities between the 1770s and the 1830s, and this was later transplanted to the Americas and then Britain during the nineteenth century. I have noticed there is a kind of fascination with ascertaining the *first* PhD, including the first in various specific contexts, and a desire to know its originary moment (although Clark's careful historical work conveys no sense of this). This may be indicative of a predilection for origins in general terms, as identified by Foucault (1991/1971), but it may also tell us something about how we imagine the PhD as coming to *be* in tandem with the birth of the research university, hence its association with the University of Berlin.

Traces of the PhD's Enlightenment origins remain in contemporary versions and accounts of the degree (Johnson *et al.*, 2000). Like any idea that has a long history, including the idea of the university itself, long-held perceptions and understandings continue to exist in contemporary iterations. The very name *Doctor of Philosophy* betrays the degree's lineage, and points to a position of status in academia – one which dates further back than 1810, and draws on long-held associations of a *philosopher* as dealing with essences in truth and knowledge (Segre, 2015). Likewise, as Barnett (2011) suggests, the idea of the scholarly university of old remains a presence in today's research and entrepreneurial university. Yet there is more to it than that: the *presence* of the old idea of the PhD is not simply a benign and nostalgic reminder of what once was; rather, it has the potential to be a disruptive force. As this book explores, the relationship between the PhD of the past and the present is evolving and shifting, and it is uneasy. There has in recent years been a certain amount of worrying away at the PhD, testing to see if it is fit for purpose *now* (Park, 2007). As others have shown (Barnacle, 2005), the last few decades have witnessed a transformation in how knowledge is conceived, and what its purpose is considered to be, which has implications for the PhD as an original contribution to knowledge. I argue here that there is a tension – a fundamental ambivalence – at the heart of the twenty-first-century idea of the PhD, which draws *both* on a valorisation of knowledge for its own sake (implicit in the title itself) *and* more contemporary utilitarian notions that it is to do with jobs and economies, the wealth of individuals and of nations. The relationship between past and present ideas is dynamic: sometimes the idea of the scholarly, Enlightenment PhD is directly challenged as irrelevant to the present, and sometimes it is nostalgically, or even mournfully, revived, as if PhD once meant something better than our contemporary understanding, and denotes something we have lost.

The PhD and the idea of the university

The appeal of the story that the PhD came to *be* with the birth of the research university shows that our ideas of the PhD – its importance or relevance to society – are closely tied to how higher education itself is understood. Ideas about the PhD are inextricable from those about the university, and its perceived purpose and function in contemporary society. Although it is an ancient institution, it is the idea of the Enlightenment university that has (albeit with localised variations) held sway in the last 200 years. The PhD degree epitomises this modern research university, and a PhD scholar signifies the 'hero of knowledge' (Johnson et al., 2000). Take Rothblatt's (2012) suggestion that the essence of a university could be discovery, knowledge, or the life of the mind: each could work equally as a definition of the PhD. Is the PhD the quintessence of the research university?

Before I get carried away with this neat definition, a caveat. The idea of the university is itself plural rather than singular, and has its roots in different histories and cultures. Each university's individual character owes much to its origins in one or other tradition, whether it springs from the idea of the modern research university in the Germanic states at the end of the eighteenth century, or the collegiate university of England in the same era (Clark, 2006; Zgaga, 2009; Segre, 2015). One of the best-known liberal conceptualisations of the university is found in Cardinal John Henry Newman's *The Idea of the University* (1871), the collection of discourses first given in the 1850s. Since that time various authors have had similar ruminations on the concept of the university. Jacques Derrida asked in a lecture in 1983 if the university had a *raison d'être* or reason to be, resulting in a pithy word play on its purpose and essence as he understood it: reason, and being (Derrida, 2004/1990). The idea (or possibilities) of the university lead to the appearance of several texts on the subject this century by Ron Barnett (2000, 2011, 2012, 2013, 2016). Different musings have prompted Rothblatt (2012) to ask if we actually need *an* idea of the university – with the admission that having one would at least give academics something to rally around.

Do we need to have *an* idea of the PhD? Like the university, which Rothblatt (2012) terms a house of many mansions in which many ideas exist, but no single idea prevails, the PhD is not limited to a single conceptualisation – although Derrida might be on to something with 'reason' and 'being'. One purpose of this book is to demonstrate the cluster of ideas around the PhD: ideas about research, knowledge and writing (Chapter 1); ideas about the kind of individual subjectivity or person who does or *is* a PhD (Chapter 2); ideas about supervision and pedagogy in the PhD (Chapter 3); and ideas about the university and the space of doctoral research (Chapter 4). Whether these really add up to a single idea, as implied by the title, may not be clarified by the end of this book (apologies to those readers who hoped it might). Yet what has become clear in the writing of this book is the extent to which our contemporary accounts and stories about the PhD still *worry away* at the idea of the Doctor of Philosophy, and the idea of the hero of knowledge, that is so closely tied to a particular historical context: the research university of the late eighteenth and early nineteenth centuries referred to above. It is not my task to *trace* the PhD (or the research university) out from its supposed point of origin, mapping its voyage to the USA, other parts of Europe, Britain and its Commonwealth, and other parts of the globe; yet I identify *traces* of that Enlightenment PhD in contemporary discourse on the doctorate in those same sites.

A PhD imaginary

It may sound like analysing traces of an idea of the PhD: a kind of Western ur-PhD implies we are in the realm of myth. In a way, we are. Perhaps PhD imaginary is a more useful term, and a better concept, taking a cue from Charles Taylor (2004). In his work on a Western social imaginary, Taylor describes an imaginary as something broad and deep, something that underpins and informs the way people *are* in relation to each other, or to a set of expectations about how things normally go. He elaborates on this further by outlining three characteristics of the social imaginary. First, the imaginary is that which ordinary people have of the social world expressed and perpetuated in stories, images and legends. The second characteristic relates to this first, in that it is not a small group of a theoretically minded minority that has in its possession this imaginary, but large numbers of ordinary folk, society as a whole. The third characteristic is that the social imaginary is collectively held, a common understanding that makes it possible for common practices to be engaged with. Taylor describes this in terms of a repertory: he gives the example of a political demonstration to show that we all have in our repertory an idea of what a demonstration is, what practices are entailed in it, the kinds of spaces where it happens, and the ways in which people relate to one another within it.

I find this a useful set of characteristics, partly as it helps delineate what this book is and is not attempting: it is not attempting to define or describe what a PhD *is* (although I will engage with some attempts to do so). What this book aims to do is argue for, and outline dimensions of, an imagined or culturally constructed PhD – a set of ideas expressed and perpetuated in stories, images and legends, held by PhD students and graduates but also in the repertory of ordinary folk or society at large, and which enable particular practices, regarded as 'normal' or how things usually go (Taylor, 2004), across diverse localised university contexts and particular institutional settings. Before continuing, I want to further underscore one of these points: what distinguishes this book from other analyses or discussions of the PhD is that it is not limited to a conceptualisation that is formed within the academy. By focusing on the stories, images and legends of society at large, as well as institutional and individual conceptualisations of the PhD within the academy, it attempts a broad *cultural* analysis of the idea of the PhD at this time.

There are a series of premises with which the book operates. The first premise is that there *is* an idea of the PhD, which could be termed a collective imaginary, that is broadly and deeply held (to echo Taylor) and which informs and enables the undertaking of the PhD at the level of institutions or individuals. The second premise subverts the first and proposes that the particular instances that articulate an idea of the PhD both shore up *and* depart or diverge from a single idea of the PhD. In other words, there is an interplay between a coherent singular, recognisable idea of the PhD, and a range of diverse things all termed PhD. This can play out as an attempt to ascertain or assert global uniformity and standardisation, such as through descriptors of the degree (like Bologna's third cycle), which sits alongside recognition of the importance of particularities, including of specific locations, disciplines, individual projects or individual researchers. Location is one of the factors that comes into play; time is another. An ahistorical idea of the PhD does not change over time. Although this is not the case with the PhD – like higher education broadly it responds to the needs of society at any given time – yet there are certain, possibly core, elements of the Enlightenment PhD that remain in contemporary versions. The contribution to knowledge and requirement for originality are ubiquitous over time and across different disciplinary contexts (Lovitts, 2007), as well as social and geographical contexts. Yet there are also aspects of the PhD that *do* change, and we are now perhaps witnessing one of the most significant of these, as it is increasingly understood in terms of its purpose and function for a global knowledge economy (KE): as a means by which institutions (or national higher education systems) compete with one another in the higher education marketplace; in terms of producing knowledge workers with skills seen as vital to the KE; and in terms of innovation via particular disciplines and fields.

The interplay between a single idea and a diversity of ideas about the PhD is recognised *and* conveyed through the makeup of this book in two main ways. First, it analyses a range of articulations of the PhD from different discourses and as found in a wide variety of texts: material analysed includes institutional descriptors, film and television series, individual researchers' stories, newspaper articles, advertisements and novels. Second, it comes at the PhD differently, enabling it to be analysed from a variety of angles. Each chapter takes one of these angles, starting with the idea of research, then the idea of the PhD researcher, to the PhD in relation to social and pedagogical contexts, and finally to the PhD as conceptualised spatially.

A central premise of this book is that the PhD imaginary is found in, and formed by, discourse and representation. There are many other ways to examine the PhD, and research literature on doctoral education this century offers examples of these, such as through focusing on the experiences of doctoral candidates in specific disciplines (Cumming, 2009b), or on supervision (Grant, 2005; Manathunga, 2014), or on the ways that PhD students talk (Mewburn, 2011). I situate this work in the context of educational research that is influenced by the discursive turn. Key elements of the discursive turn as it impacts on educational research are outlined by MacLure (2003), including that the idea of *text* is central to an analytical project that focuses on discourse. By text I mean both a *thing* in the form of a piece of writing or a visual text, and more flexible kind of structure which is fundamentally social (Bakhtin, 1975), relational (Barthes, 1977) and open, rather than bounded (McGann, 1991). Another of MacLure's claims is that language and reality – words and things – are entangled in ways that are difficult to fully account for. Throughout this book the analysis of the PhD operates primarily at the level of the textual. Nonetheless, there is a recognition that representation and reality bear some relation to each other, whether it is a tricky imbrication or layering, or a complex and complicated knot. There is also a recognition of what the textual cannot capture or what exceeds it, particularly as relating to the bodily experiences of individual researchers. The imagined and the lived are intertwined about and inform one another, but not in ways that are straightforward. The gap between words and things is productive (Foucault, 1994/1970; MacLure, 2003) and at certain points in each chapter this book hovers on the edge of this very space. While I acknowledge the limits of the discursive, I nonetheless consider that there has been insufficient attention given (even since 'the turn') to language and discourse in educational research – and *higher* education research is no exception. In this era, perhaps more than ever, we need to pay attention to the power of discourse and representation, which means attention to discourses 'outside' the university or higher educational context, including, among other things, literary and popular culture.

Whose culture?

If there is an idea of the PhD that this book traces and engages with, sometimes problematizing, it is a Western cultural idea. It is the PhD which spread over 200 years from Germany to other parts of Europe, the USA, the United Kingdom (UK) and the Commonwealth, and it is primarily from these latter contexts that I have gathered my sources. It is therefore mainly – but not solely – an analysis of a Western and Anglophone idea of the PhD. The texts that I analyse all come from New Zealand (NZ), Australia, the UK, Canada and the United States of America (USA). Although this provides the book with a manageable scope, some readers will find it a limitation. One justification for the focus is that the discursive terrain in these sites is so rich: there is a proliferation of represented (not to mention *actual*) PhDs in these contexts. The sheer scale indicates a need to critically examine these representations, to consider *why* it is that the PhD engenders such broad cultural interest, now, at this moment of the early twenty-first century. To reframe a question that Flint and Peim (2012) ask of childhood: what is the significance of the current obsession with the PhD?

The proliferation of PhDs in discourse, and the scale of interest, highlights a need to deconstruct the PhD as it is currently (over)represented, to enable critical examination of it, and to forestall the entrenchment of a single monolithic idea. The cluster of accounts in the twentieth century of *intertextuality*, or the interaction and engagement between different texts (even those produced in quite different contexts), is helpful here. As Bakhtin (1981) has shown, texts are social in that they 'talk' to each other and borrow from one another: they are fundamentally intertextual (Kristeva, 1995). Current accounts of the PhD endlessly borrow from each other, and from older stories, reworking and reconfiguring existing ideas. This can give rise, as this book explores, to interesting contradictions.

Looking awry at the PhD

An aim of this book, then, is to critically analyse contemporary discourse on the PhD. One dimension that assists with this task (and with destabilising norms) is an interdisciplinary element, as I draw on methods of data collection and analysis from more than one disciplinary field. Interdisciplinary research has been described as risky, in that all the unknowns of one's own subject area are combined with the uncertainties of another (Cronon, 1983). This book pushes that risk further, as there are three disciplines that have influenced this study – higher education, English or literary studies, and history. This results partly from a quirk of who I am as a scholar, how my academic predilections were formed through undergraduate and post-graduate work, and in my subsequent roles as an academic. I cannot resist doing historical work and literary analysis, despite being a higher education scholar. The primary reason, however, for the mash-up that is this book, and I mean this in the sense of the musical mash-up of different songs and musical genres rather than a culinary mash, is that working across disciplinary borders enables us to *look at the objects of study differently* rather than through a single lens, which courts normativity. Since late last century, social and educational theorists have called for more across disciplines and paradigms to ensure that the grand narratives, and a *making sense* tendency in research, do not settle and solidify. I agree that this kind of research work is both risky (particularly in the sense of being dismissed by purveyors of 'gold-standard' research (Lather, 2006)) and unsettling. Traditionally, educational researchers distance themselves (and their work) from associations with the literary – although they are much happier with being associated with history – a consequence, MacLure (2003) argues, of claims to seriousness, and to truth. Fiction is slippery, tends to resist truth, and happily embraces contradictions; these are not characteristics of serious research. And yet, to work with contradictions as possible sites of action *is* the goal of a critical scholar of education (Apple, 2006), and to unsettle or disrupt *is* the function of theory, according to Gulson and Parkes (2010), who suggest that bringing theory to doctoral research denaturalises, diffracts and deconstructs. Interestingly, Gulson and Parkes then give the example of not theory, but *fiction*, used by Noel Gough (1998) to denaturalise (plus those other 'de' words above) the science curriculum. I agree with their suggestion that fictional narratives share the disruptive bent of theory on whatever object comes under their gaze, and share this aim. In this book I look at the PhD, the object of the gaze of this book, somewhat awry.[1]

Why now? Current imaginaries

Some unsettlement in the matter of the PhD is timely. Arguably, there is one particular imaginary that, in certain (primarily institutional and governmental) discursive settings, holds sway, and that is the neoliberal imaginary for the PhD, or the idea that its central purpose is to contribute to the KE. Although the market has always to some extent exerted its influence on academia (Clark, 2006), since the late twentieth-century changes to higher education have impacted on the governance, funding and the curriculum in universities so that, as noted by Barnett (1994) in an early work, they are experiencing a seismic shift not in the ways they operate but in how their core purpose is understood and articulated. The idea of the university, according to Shore (2010), has morphed from the university as a place of critical enquiry and independent learning, to a transnational business corporation competing in the global KE. Barnett (2013) claims that the idea of the research university which has held sway since the nineteenth century has given way to the entrepreneurial and corporate university. Although, as indicated, the purpose of the university may not ever have been singularly understood (Rothblatt, 1997; Collini, 2008; Segre, 2015), the contemporary idea that it has a core function to contribute to a global KE is currently ubiquitous. It may be the case that the lack of a singular, unifying conceptualisation of the university (Rothblatt's (2012) house of many mansions) has rendered it particularly vulnerable to this reconfiguration: in the absence of a coherent (or grand) twenty-first-century narrative that might give meaning to education, *efficiency* has become key (Flint and Peim, 2012).

Taylor's (2004) account of a social imaginary is useful here, as I think it helps us understand the ways in which a particular theory or ideology like neoliberalism can infiltrate and transform an imaginary. It is through *practices*, Taylor suggests, that the imaginary is transformed, as people take up new practices, improvise them, or are inducted into new ones. The neoliberal turn in universities can be seen in this way: as Shore (2010) and others have shown, the practices of managerialism have done their part in shifting the ways in which universities not only function but are *understood*. According to Taylor (2004), new practices only make sense according to the new 'outlook' or idea – this idea then provides the context in which the practices make sense. Gradually, the new way of thinking, together with the new ways of doing, begin to define the contours of our world and eventually form a shape of things that becomes taken for granted, or too obvious to note (Taylor, 2004).

In a way, the PhD was a sitting duck (a feral one at that) for the introduction of the new practices of managerialism under a neoliberal ideology. As it requires an original contribution to knowledge, the PhD was perfectly placed to appeal to the idea of higher education and research as furthering the KE. Further, as an independent and self-directed course of study, with no real, in the sense of enforced, determinants regarding a fixed completion time, nor a highly determined form, other than a thesis of around 100,000 words, it seemed ripe for doing over by well-meaning educationalists *and* administrators bent on improving efficiencies and outputs. The trussed up rigorous version of the PhD, complete with set goals, predetermined meeting schedules, supervisor/

student agreements, how-to writing guides and workshops, a fixed completion time, often attendant with rewards or punishments, may have wrought some advantageous changes, not least of which has been a demystification; yet it has also engendered a change of the kind Taylor describes, whereby the contours of the 'thing itself' are increasingly determined by the practices put in place to manage it. New practices, or modifications of old ones, gradually change the meanings of our imaginaries, and so profound transformations occur without us even being fully aware that they are happening (Taylor, 2004).

In universities, a transformation of this kind is occurring; what is interesting about the cultural imaginary of the PhD, in its broadest iteration, is that the sea change is made visible. In the cultural imaginary of the PhD, 'old' ideas and 'new' ideas – including accounts of current practices and former practices – butt up against each other in ways that highlight connections and disparities. To make a different (albeit related) point, it is precisely because there *is* a sea change occurring that we see such a proliferation of engagements in contemporary culture with the idea of the PhD. Fiction, literature, the novel, popular culture are barometers of change – signalling epistemic ruptures – as critical theorists of literature and culture have long asserted (Burke, 1953; Belsey, 1980; Bakhtin, 1981; Hutcheon, 1999).

A word on practices and things

A limitation of a book that focuses on analysing representations is its lack of engagement with the work that is the 'real thing' of the PhD. The activities involved in doing research (Cumming, 2009a, 2009b), the hard slog of the mundane reality of research in day-to-day terms, might seem distant from the airiness and insubstantiality of an imagined or discursive construction. Although there is some discussion of the *work* of doing a PhD, I make no claims to situate this research within the frame of the 'practice turn' in doctoral education research (Boud and Lee 2009); yet nor do I see the discursive and the material as being quite as antithetical as others have, Schatzki included (2002), or as occupying entirely different theoretical universes. At the very least, practices, people and things and the interactions and relationships between them are represented in discourse – including, in research literature, about educational practices (Cumming, 2009b; Hopwood, 2014). Nonetheless, the *outside* of representation is not my focus in this book, although I acknowledge its existence. Bennett (2001) writes of 'thing-power' or the capacity of things to resist the frame of cultural construction, which is an idea I come back to in Chapter 1, in considering encounters with things in research that resist complying with a doctoral researcher's frame of knowledge.

There are wildernesses in research – terrains that cannot be mapped, dissected and known – and I recognise that these exist here, on the edges of this book, as much as they do for the PhD researchers I write about. The out-side that Bennett (2001) describes is occasionally met with, gestured toward, but it is not (cannot be) brought into the frame.

Stories and images of the PhD

In the chapters that follow, I trace ideas of the PhD in the form of accounts, stories, myths and images from various sources. I attempt to balance thorough analysis of particular texts (to deconstruct an idea) with conveying the scope and variety of representations in the cultural imaginary of the PhD (to demonstrate its ubiquity). The cultural practices (novels, television shows, plays and films) date from the end of the twentieth century onwards, from NZ, Australia, the UK, Canada and the USA. Ideas of the PhD produced by research participants are from graduates from around 2000 onwards, or enrolled PhDs at the time of the research. They are derived from written accounts, images that represent the PhD, or other textual material that the participants offered me, including drawings, photographs of their workspaces, pieces of data (excluding research data involving other participants) and reflections. The written accounts were responses to a request to write about their *idea of the PhD* and include a mix of imaginings and memories of their own experience: in some instances, these were supplemented by interviews to clarify or amplify elements of the written texts. Throughout the book I refer to these data variously as participant accounts, texts or written imaginings and I think of them as versions of the *petit recits* that Lyotard (1993/1979) suggests counter the grand narratives of traditional Western historical discourse. They are little in the sense of being individualistic or personal, arising from lived experience and the imagination. They are not always polished, crafted and *finished*; they are not quite fragment-texts, but nor are they edited published texts; and while some tell a story, few conform to a strict narrative shape, with a beginning, middle and end.

Like the stories about supervision that Grant (2005) describes, the *petit recits* that the research participants produced have a genealogy and are contributed to by older stories. To put it another way, they are part of a broader discourse about the PhD, about universities, writing and research, that informs them and which they too inform, in disruptive ways, as well as through reaffirming existing imaginaries. Stories have a social life (Cruikshank, 1998) and provide a framework for making sense of the world through utilising a form of narrative that is shared: this idea is echoed in Taylor's (2004) thesis of a social imaginary. Times of fracture or rapid change can be countered by a return to old stories, Cruikshank (1998) writes, to provide continuity and a reassuring sense of order, and to subvert orthodoxies or newly conventional ways of thinking. Perhaps we tell old stories and tall stories, familiar and well-worn stories, troubling and uncanny stories and ideas about the PhD to counter the current discourse that highlights the bland utility and *usefulness* of the PhD for national and global knowledge economies. Here I analyse some of these ideas and stories.

Endnote

1 Thanks to Slavoj Žižek and William Shakespeare for this phrase.

CHAPTER 1

The nature of doctoral research

> The university proper is a small academic institution. Its animating purpose is to discover things . . . This task was organised as a quest for truth.
>
> (Murphy, 2015)

> That was what I planned to do – to hunt the elusive Pink Carnation through the archives of England, to track down any sliver of long-dead gossip that might lead me to what the finest minds in the French government had failed to discover. Of course, that wasn't how I phrased it when I suggested the idea to my dissertation advisor. I made scholarly noises about filling a gap in the historiography, and the deep sociological significance of spying as a means of asserting manhood, and other silly ideas couched in intellectual unintelligibility. I called it 'Aristocratic Espionage during the Wars with France: 1789-1815'. Rather a dry title, but somehow I doubt 'Why I Love Men in Black Masks' would have made it past my dissertation committee.
>
> (Willig, 2005: 3)

Stories about doing a PhD in the cultural domain highlight the idea of *discovery* as central to a PhD imaginary. As others have shown (Brew, 2001; Murphy, 2015), the idea of discovery is also bound up with a broadly held understanding of the animating purpose of the university itself. As the stories analysed in this chapter show, a research discovery or find can happen in any number of research settings, from archaeological or historic sites to laboratories, or while sitting at a desk in a university library. What varying accounts of *doing* research share, and this also refers to writing the thesis, is the idea that the aim of research is to uncover something new or hitherto unknown, to produce something original.

Doctoral research is understood both as a set of activities or practices (as *doing*) and as a contribution to knowledge, usually in the form of the completed thesis (as a *thing*). While a concept of originality is fundamental to how the contribution to knowledge is imagined, along with knowledge of the existing field of research literature, contemporary understandings otherwise vary and are contested. As Brew (2001) outlines, research can be seen as a commodity, as learning or as teaching, as discourse, as scholarship or as knowledge. Whereas institutional views of doctoral research emphasise originality and significance, and continue to draw on the idea of the PhD as increasing disciplinary knowledge (Barnacle, 2005), they are also impacted on by government policies, which tend to highlight the contributions of innovative research to national economies and to building the national research capacity. The aim and purpose of research articulated in non-institutional discourse, in contemporary cultural imaginings, tend *not* to highlight economic or national gains of research (although there are exceptions), but instead revert to what might be considered more traditional view of knowledge as *for its own sake*. Is this part of our inheritance from the Enlightenment PhDs? Yes, and no. In this chapter we will see that the contemporary cultural imaginary of the PhD also draws on ideas of knowledge which predate the PhD itself, recalling pre-Enlightenment notions of knowledge-seeking as risky, unorthodox and as challenging dominant orders of knowledge.

At the heart of the challenge to contemporary institutional and government notions of what research constitutes is the idea of *mystery*. In popular culture, mystery offers a counterpoint to a utilitarian focus on research, for instance, as a contribution to the economy or in terms of skills-development: it also constitutes another less direct challenge to a modern idea of research based on rationality, by illustrating not only that there are things which cannot be mastered, but also the contingency of attempts to fully define (or again, master) knowledge itself. The disappearance of mystery from the university, or what Barnett (2011), channelling Max Weber, terms the disenchantment with enchantment in the modern university, is an idea that cultural conceptualisations of the PhD engage with, and resist, as this chapter considers. Mystery is not absent from contemporary stories about doctoral research, by researchers or in cultural practices, even if it is (entirely) absent from formal institutional descriptors of research. In contemporary imaginaries of the doctorate there is the presence of the *other* to rational Enlightenment knowledge, and charisma, luck and chance are part of research method as it is popularly understood.

Alongside that idea, sometimes countering it, sometimes not, is a conceptualisation of research as *busy* work by an individual researcher-student: as activities (Cumming, 2009b) and doing. In literary and popular culture, research often involves a group of scientists clustered around a bench, or a dig, working at something (like bones or remains) with implements – not always the right kind of implements, according to actual scientists. In the written accounts of PhD research by participants in my study, a few included detailed descriptions of this busy work, including Bronwyn Lloyd (Art History), who wrote of working in the archive transcribing in her twelve 'mad' notebooks with sharp pencils, and of marginalia 'where [she] tracked the clues'. Accounts of research activities, practices and methods, as this chapter considers, are bound up with ideas of mystery and discovery.

Even so, that idea of the production of original research remains a foundational characteristic of the PhD, which betrays its origins. The idea that knowledge should be original or *new* was itself once a fairly novel idea, according to our understanding of the history of the university. In early modern European universities, the close alliance between church and university meant that the idea that scholars could or should produce something truly original was unorthodox, and could be seen to pose a heretical threat to holy writ (Segre, 2015). Discovery may have been one aim of the university, as Murphy (2015) argues, but it was understood in terms of scholarship on existing knowledge, rather than producing *new* knowledge (Brew, 2001). The dominant narrative of the university tells us that truth was considered to be fixed, unchanging, and encounters with anomalies were deeply unsettling to the order of things (Foucault, 1994/1970; Daston and Park, 2001; Segre, 2015). According to this narrative, that did not stop certain scholars from trying to exceed the orthodox, and stories of those who did dare, including fictional figures like Faust or Victor Frankenstein, or historical figures such as Galileo, who pushed beyond the boundaries of the known, rarely prospered, were ostracised by church and university, and so served to warn others who might be similarly tempted to overreach. It is only in the last 200 years that a contribution to knowledge came to be valued as original, and its contributors celebrated as heroes (Clark, 2006; Murphy, 2015).

Universities worldwide write this idea of originality into institutional statute. Although originality can mean different things in different disciplinary contexts, there is nonetheless, according to Lovitts (2007), a shared idea that it denotes something *new*. To produce original research, the doctoral researcher needs certain qualities (considered further in Chapter 2) or characteristics like curiosity and creativity, and an appreciation for discovery. These terms are echoed in a study of academics' perceptions of research conducted by Brew (2001), who found that one of the ways in which academics experience research involves the discovery of underlying meanings and the bringing to light of ideas – that old Enlightenment association of light and truth (Derrida, 1982/1972). Similarly, in Meyer *et al.* (2005), ways that postgraduate students described research included the discovery of truth, a process of exploration and discovery, and the uncovering of what has been hidden. The language of *discovery* and finding truth recurs again and again in our stories about doctoral research.

Research as discovery

Literary and popular culture draws on, and contributes to, this idea that research is a process of tracking or locating clues, as described by novelist Lauren Willig (2005) or research participant Bronwyn Lloyd, leading to the revelation of a truth; or that the goal of a research project is to make a unique discovery, or solve a puzzle, and graduate researchers are like detectives or 'truth-seekers' (Lloyd, 1984, quoted in Johnson et al., 2000). I want to examine this particular idea about research in two literary texts: Elizabeth Kostova's popular gothic tale *The Historian* (2005) and Rebecca Gowers' lesser-known *The Twisted Heart: A Literary Murder Mystery and a Tale of Modern Love* (2009), both of which have central characters who are doctoral research students. Both novels also draw on the conventions of the crime or detective genre (although there are other genres, like the gothic, also at play) and depict research as a process of amassing clues – clues that will eventually lead to uncovering the truth. Other cultural texts alluded to in this book also make this connection between research and detective work, including the TV crime series *Bones*, Antonia Susan (A.S.) Byatt's academic detective novel *Possession: A Romance* (1990) and *The Biographer's Tale* (2000), Willig's (2005) *The Secret History of the Pink Carnation* and Rachael King's *Magpie Hall* (2009).

The researcher in *The Twisted Heart*, Kit, is doing a DPhil at Oxford in nineteenth-century English literature, researching a number of different strands relating to Victorian crime, real and fictional. Kit is also teaching a course on one of the first detective novels, Dickens' *Bleak House*, and is preoccupied with murder in Dickens' *Oliver Twist*. The connections between her research, her real work, as she terms it, and teaching become stronger as the novel progresses, as Kit follows up on an article in *The Dickensian* she had 'stumbled on' while preparing the course reading list. Seated in her favourite seat, Kit becomes discouraged and wonders how exhaustive her thesis research really needs to be. Is she following a link that is too tenuous in reading about the murder of Eliza Grimwood? Yet it soon turns out that this *is* Kit's real work, as she begins to realize. With further research, Kit discovers that not only did Dickens write of the Grimwood murder in *Household Words*, he also used it as the basis for Sikes' murder of Nancy in *Oliver Twist*, which becomes Kit's most significant discovery and the original contribution that her thesis will make.

Instinct is how Kit describes the initial lead, which becomes a puzzle she wants to solve. Research in this novel is a combination of luck or chance – Kit stumbles on important facts – and method. Kit is practical and thorough and follows up every clue, even if it seems unrelated, and she keeps a notebook (like Bronwyn Lloyd) in which she records everything. Gradually, the seemingly random clues start to form a pattern and the two strands of Kit's work that had seemed separate – her teaching and research – come together. The novel overcomes two traditional binaries by recombining not only *chance* and *method* in Kit's research, but also *teaching* and *research*.

Chance and method are similarly employed by the researchers in Kostova's (2005) novel. The historian of the title refers to Paul, the doctoral student writing a dissertation on Dutch merchants; Paul's supervisor Rossi, a charismatic history professor; and Helen, a doctoral student in anthropology. The narrative begins with a series of seemingly serendipitous events – a book suddenly appears on the library carrel of Paul, who is then drawn, initially by curiosity, into a different field of research – the main purpose of which is to locate the legendary tomb of Dracula and his advisor, Rossi, whom the vampire has kidnapped. The search for Rossi is presented throughout the novel as research, and like Kit in *The Twisted Heart*, the characters in this novel learn that the subject of historical research is real, not simply the stuff of books, but 'terrible' and true. Although research is revered in the novel, it is also depicted as unhealthy: Rossi tells Paul that anyone who pokes around in history for too long could well go insane. The archives are hallowed and cloister-like, a haven for scholars, but also threatening and corrupted, and even life-negating. This dimension of the archive is a recurring idea in imaginings of PhD research, as Chapter 4 considers.

The research process described in *The Historian* combines several methods. The first involves recognisable scholarly activity: archival searching, analysis of primary sources and other texts, interviews, and checking or cross-referencing sources. Paul describes the careful methods in which he has been trained as a respect for order and thoroughness that overlooks nothing, neither a single document nor an archive, regardless of its location. Other methods are less rational, but perhaps no less recognisable. One is chance encounter, a form that Rossi and Paul have little respect for, but nonetheless experience: Rossi calls research a chase after a 'random sign' in a book stumbled across by accident. The other is the experience of a scholar's intuition – trusted only when backed up by careful work – or a nagging at the back of the mind (Kostova, 2009), like the instinct described by Kit.

The aim of research in Kostova's novel is, through a combination of these methods, to bring things to light that might be relevant to the research, and to collect clues. By equating light for insight or knowledge, and dark for ignorance or unknowing, Kostova draws on that common trope in Western culture (Derrida, 1982/1972) that consistently reappears in accounts of doctoral research in fiction *and* in studies of academics' perceptions of research

(Brew, 2001; Akerlind, 2008). Research is also seen to involve a need to satisfy curiosity – but can also contain an element of competitiveness: Helen's aim initially is to be the first to publish and to know more than anyone else about Dracula legends. However, the search for Rossi becomes something else for Helen: a search for understanding of her own origins and the truth about her birth.

In both these novels, research is represented as a process of following clues, being thorough, unravelling puzzles, following instinct, and achieving resolution. The resolution at the close of each involves the solving of the mystery (who did it?) *and* completion of the research project. At the end of Gowers' novel, adversary is overcome in a way that suits both the mystery-novel and the romance: the truth that Kit discovers is both research related (history was real) and personal (love is real) – like the discovery made by the scholars at the end of Byatt's *Possession: A Romance* (1990) which similarly combines academic detective fiction with romance. In Kostova's novel, however, the initially neat resolution is undermined by an unsettling epilogue in which we learn that Helen dies soon after she is reunited with her family, and that Dracula himself may not be safely dead after all, but up to his old tricks of leaving scary books for scholars to find in library carrels. *The Historian's* allegiance to more than one genre further unsettles the resolution implied by the (initial) end. As an academic crime story, the researcher-detectives apply a methodical and rational approach to research – but they meet their match when the mystery they try to solve turns out to belong to the realm of horror and the gothic, and to involve the supernatural. As the novel draws on more than one genre, it cannot provide a neat ending such as Gowers is able to in her work of straightforward academic crime fiction.

The application of reasoned method to a problem is as fundamental to detective work (as it is presented in fiction) as it is to scientific inquiry. Indeed, the relationship between literature and science is a long-held one, according to some scholars (Beer, 2000). King (2005) points out that before crime fiction, the nineteenth-century realist novel drew on the same ideas about the existence of objective truths as Victorian sciences. Both held that observation of the world (natural or social) could give rise to *objective* knowledge, and therefore further progress – George Eliot's realist fiction is a case in point. More specifically, novels about *crime* have evolved, according to Belsey (1980), as a result of the status accorded to science: stories that begin in mystery conclude with a logical explanation, making it clear that any mystery can be made accountable to reason through deduction and scientific method. In the educational context, Gough (2010) has argued for intertextual continuity between detective fiction and narratives of educational inquiry, not least because research resembles detective stories insofar as both are narrative quests to determine 'the truth' about something. Gough raises the possibility of teaching methodological approaches using detective fiction, to encourage research students to compare their own research methods with those of fictional detectives as a way of contrasting research paradigms.

The idea is not simply that fictional research resembles real research (or vice versa) but that both arise from certain assumptions about what knowledge is. Gough (2010) draws on the idea that texts in quite different contexts can resemble each other because both are produced within what Hayles (1990) describes as the same cultural field. The phenomenon of different disciplines being drawn to explore similar problems can be accounted for, Hayles (1990) suggests, because the underlying concerns are determined by the cultural context, or because they are constructed on assumptions about knowledge in the given episteme. How might we characterise the twenty-first century episteme? In 1994, Barnett predicted that new knowledge paradigms would be needed in twenty-first-century education other than those that privilege truth and objective knowledge, because not only is what counts as truth debatable, now, but the idea of objective knowledge has largely been abandoned, even if some still 'hanker' after it (Barnett, 1994). Late twentieth-century postmodern academic fictions, such as those by Byatt and David Lodge display both a suspicion of universal concepts, including truth, and a longing (Barnett's 'hankering') for them. According to Barnett, in higher education the loss of faith in truth has engendered a seismic shift at a conceptual as well as an operational level in the tertiary arena (2000). This shift is what Gough (2010) refers to when he claims that recent transformations in detective fiction *and* educational inquiry are not only comparable but are intertextually linked because they are manifestations of the cultural and discursive shifts of postmodernity. Both participate in the same cultural field, to borrow Hayles' (1990) term.

According to Gough (2010), postmodern detective fictions draw on the conventions of detective fiction yet do not resuscitate an 'old' idea of truth. He describes the 'anti-detectives' of postmodern crime fiction and suggests these are more appropriate models for emerging educational researchers than conventional fictional detectives. After post-structuralism, he argues, it is no longer defensible to conduct educational research like a conventional detective. In what is almost a reversal of my argument here, Gough (2010) contends that for the most part educational research still privileges the rationalism associated with the sciences, while detective fiction does not. To some extent, the opposition between Gough's argument and mine is less of a contradiction than an indication of the range of genres within detective fiction. Indeed, Gough refers to this range when he compares hard-boiled crime fiction with more classic forms as a way of highlighting *different* paradigms within educational research. Unlike the more experimental texts that Gough discusses, in recent versions of academic fiction that draw on the conventions of classic detective fiction, the discovery of truth is both a possibility and the central aim of the scholarly detectives. The detective-researchers in academic fiction are arch-detectives, rather than anti-detectives, who know how to exercise their capacity for reason.

The capacities displayed by Kit, Paul and Helen – all of whom are successful or 'good' postgraduate researchers in the sense that they solve the mystery, finish the thesis and achieve personal resolution – are contingent on their autonomous *use of reason*: they are able to make judgements independently. We are back with Derrida's (2004) *reason* and *being*. Through the course of completing the research project they have demonstrated a reliance on rational thought, which is privileged over such dubious attributes as genius (Yeatman, 1998) or charisma (Clark, 2006; Lee and Green, 2009) and instinct. This opposition is not always maintained, however, and terms like these are reverted to by way of explanation in these fictional texts – as they sometimes are by academics and research students (see Brew, 2001; Meyer *et al.*, 2005; Akerlind, 2008).

Significantly, the independence and autonomy of the researcher must be negotiated through a relationship with the supervisor. In *The Historian*, the absence of his supervisor forces Paul, the graduate student, to act independently: initially, Paul struggles with his unwanted autonomy and constantly defers to his supervisor before finally realizing his potential and assuming true independence. In an Oedipal twist, once the newly autonomous Paul, together with Helen, finds 'Father Rossi' he realizes they must actually kill him, as he has been infected by Dracula, in order to save him. By making Rossi cross over to Dracula's side (albeit unwillingly), Kostova underscores that he is the Other against which Paul's self must be determined (Hall, 1996). Dracula has forced Rossi to become supernatural, so that he too is outside of the realm of what is good, reasoned and rational (and alive), and has shifted to the side of the unknowable (and the dead) against which Helen and Paul have pitted themselves. As Hall (1996) has described, the self/other relation is usually posited along the lines of binary oppositions. In these novels, the researcher-self that succeeds in the end is constructed as the rational and autonomous Enlightenment subject who exercises reason, and applies order and logic. Nonetheless, these individuals do occasionally succumb to relying on luck, instinct and charisma.

In these works of contemporary fiction, the 'seeker after truth' metaphor for the postgraduate researcher is alive and well. Far from providing new conceptions of doctoral study, new modes of knowledge production such as Barnett describes (1994, 2000) seem to have inspired a re-inscription in fiction of the more traditional figure of the scholar defined by Johnson *et al.* (2000).

Both parts of this metaphor, 'seeker' and 'truth', sit at odds with the outcomes often emphasized in institutional constructions of postgraduate researchers, such as skills and capacities that knowledge workers gain, and with what is currently constructed as knowledge in higher education (Barnett, 1994).

There is a third term, bound up with conceptions of truth and seeker, that also merits consideration: the university. Although this will be the focus of Chapter 4, I want to highlight here that the university in these two texts – the *space* that the imagined seeker after truth inhabits – is one that allows for the kind of research activity he or she undertakes, with darkened archives, library carrels, and lonely rooms that facilitate the bringing to light of new truths, or long-hidden truths, as in the case of historical research. The darkness in these two novels also contains elements of threat and violence that disturbs the orderly surface of the university: Kit describes Oxford as an ivory 'horror show' rather than an ivory tower (Gowers, 2009). Her Oxford is a grittier, sometimes violent world of pubs, fights in alleys and petty gangsters. In *The Historian*, the threat is of a supernatural kind, not easily overcome with reason and orderly conduct, which has penetrated to the cloistered heart of the university, the archive. Kostova demonstrates that resuscitating the past in the search for truth is not without risks: her characters are warned against pursuing avenues of historical research in case something is stirred up which cannot be contained.

Saltmarsh (2009) has described the potential of haunting as a conceptual tool to examine relationships between the past, present and future *and* to unsettle the ideological truths of the present. Drawing on the work of Derrida, Saltmarsh suggests that through the use of the conceptual tool of haunting, our accepted rationalities can be interrogated *by* those very (other) forms of knowledge which have been silenced, relegated to the margins, or cast into history. Research encounters then become a means, she argues, by which spectral moments of intervention can take place (Saltmarsh, 2009). Haunting is a dominant motif in academic crime fictions that have doctoral detectives as characters: the victims of unsolved murders seek justice and resolution, or recognition, not to mention the occasional appearance of the ultimate figure of the un-dead, Dracula. These hauntings do more than fulfil readers' expectations of gothic crime fiction, however. They also serve to interrogate ideas about truth and the purpose of research, reinstating mystery and challenging the neoliberal rationalities of our present.

Research as collection: orders of things

In the contemporary PhD imaginary, *collection* is another form of doctoral research. Like the doctoral detective, the figure of the researcher-as-collector is also a seeker, of sorts. Whereas the research students in the above narratives seek to uncover a truth that solves a mystery, researcher-collectors seek to find something unique or unexamined. Collecting is also a form of puzzle-solving in that a collection of something presents us with an extensive array, possibly even a totality, of the given thing which facilitates our understanding of it – including understanding of its variety or complexity. So one aspect of collecting is the amassing of something, the forming of a set, so as to examine it. For the collection to be extensive, the researcher needs to be thorough, to explore any likely sources or places, although accidental discoveries also advance the project. Collections require parameters, to have limits and to define the characteristics of the items within them, and there needs to be an organising principle that enables things to be defined against each other and arranged, not higgledy-piggledy. Collection is primarily conceived of as a rational activity, although it can tip over into obsession and desire. Although this is a contemporary idea of doctoral research, there are historical precedents which date back to the first doctorates in the early nineteenth-century.

In his discussion of the Doctor of Philosophy and the rise of the modern research university in the early nineteenth-century German states, Clark (2006) describes the popularity of certain dissertation topics (often in relation to advisor preferences), including the 'prosopographical doctoral dissertation'. This type of research focused on an often unknown or 'obscure' classical scholar and assembled all 'traces' relating to that scholar. Altogether the aim of these dissertations was to contribute to knowledge of antiquity scholarship through the collection of classical fragments, it was a type of doctoral research project ubiquitous at the time, but which was not unanimously supported as a useful endeavour. As Clark describes, an anonymous article appeared in 1817 entitled 'Is It Advisable to Encourage Young Philologists to Collect Fragments?' The author of the article questions the value of such a painstaking task on an 'obscure' writer as a doctoral project. An advantage of this kind of scholarship was that the doctoral candidates, in order to be assured that they had *found* all possible 'hiding' fragments, became acquainted with a broad variety of sources. This was the opinion of Professor Ritschl, in 1835, who gave a series of lectures on classical philology and who defended the collection of fragments as an appropriate task for German scholars that benefited both the scholar, who gained extensive knowledge of a range of texts, and scholarship (Clark, 2006). The collection of fragments is an exhaustive approach to research, a method that enables a foundation of knowledge on a given topic to be established and able to be ordered. One of the dissertations Clark refers to, produced in 1831 in Berlin, attempted to reconstruct Greek folk songs.

The thesis-collection of folk songs recalls the contemporaneous and better-known project of the brothers Jacob and Wilhelm Grimm to collect and preserve Germanic folk tales. They were both associated with universities, and Clark's book includes a drawing by Ludwig Grimm of Jacob giving a seminar at Göttingen in 1830. The Grimms' project was to record in writing, and thus preserve, the oral folk tales of the German countries. The gradual privileging of *writing* over the oral and aural in universities at this time, which Clark suggests reaches its apotheosis in the doctoral dissertation, infers that the Grimms' collection is part of a broader shift away from oral traditions, in which folk tales are both more ephemeral and also more variant, to a written tradition in which tales are preserved, ordered and subject to a kind of uniformity. Like the classical fragments of the prosopographical thesis, the exhaustive nature of the Grimms' collection of folk tales infers provision of a full set, enabling knowledge and understanding of folk tales. *Unlike* the classical fragments, the Grimms' collected tales were not based on textual fragments, and their tellers were often ordinary women who occupied domestic (although not always lower class, as is popularly believed) settings, rather than scholarly men. The Grimms' project – like the thesis of Greek folk ditties – in some respects runs counter to emerging ideas about what constituted worthy or appropriate topics to pursue for research. The debates that Clark refers to indicate that from the outset there was disagreement over what was acceptable, what constituted a PhD. Folklore and fantastic tales belong to the category of the marvellous, or even the vulgar, and were not the credible objects of inquiry primarily valued by Enlightenment scholars, as Daston and Park (2001) outline. On the other hand, the Grimms' project could be seen as an attempt to bring folk tales into line – to make them credible, or tidy them up into moral allegories.

Referencing these Enlightenment predecessors is a contemporary story (in which the collection of traditional folk tales as research for a doctorate forms the plot) in a recent Scottish play in verse, by David Greig and Wils Wilson, performed 2011–13 by the National Theatre of Scotland. In *The Strange Undoing of Prudencia Hart*, the title character is an academic and doctoral candidate working on a thesis entitled 'Paradigms of Emotional Contact in The Performance and Text of Traditional Folk Song in Scotland 1572–1798'. This was according to the promotional material, although in performances the topic was given more pithily as 'The Topography of Hell in Scottish Balladry' (2013). The dates of Prudencia's source texts inform us that her project is focused on pre-Enlightenment folk tales. Further, the end date reminds us of the *decline* of folk tales after this era, as written forms of storytelling gradually eclipsed oral, and as the subjects of these tales, the fantastic and marvellous, diminished in popularity (Dalston and Park, 2001).

The dates also indicate Prudencia's aim to collect a *set* of tales, her data, within the parameters of an historical period and cultural and geographical locale. As a thorough, and somewhat traditional, researcher, Prudencia should have as extensive a collection as possible of Border folk tales. In this, she is contrasted with her fellow researchers in the play, who undertake more fashionable projects with contemporary methodologies, underpinned by late twentieth- century conceptualisations of knowledge. At a conference in Kelso, Prudencia participates in a panel discussion on folk with colleagues Colin Symes, who analyses football chants as modern-day folk, in a cultural studies project, and Master's student Seoligha, who is undertaking a poststructuralist analysis of folk. Prudencia is more like her own father, who collected vinyl records which he endlessly ordered and catalogued to the point of obsession. Like her father, she quests for that rare thing that will make her set complete: the ballad never before collected – something that no one else has captured, something unique.

Initially, Prudencia is characterised as highly organised and methodical as a researcher. The cost of being so focused on her work, on her quest, as Prudencia laments in the ladies' room of the pub in Kelso, is that she is restrained, an observer rather than a participant in life – not able to join in with songs and tales but only to watch others, to take notes and observe. While at the conference, Prudencia hears of the existence of the original song, an uncollected ballad, and she sets out to find it. However, that night Prudencia falls into a ballad of her own and gets taken by the Devil, a frightening yet charismatic Lucifer figure in the tradition of Milton, who is himself a collector of books, and souls, like Dracula in Kostova's novel. Eventually, once she escapes the Devil's clutches, Prudencia is able at last to sing a ballad of her own, to choose *life* not books, shifting her position from collector of folk tales, to maker of and participant in a tale. The strange and wonderful thing that happens to Prudencia occurs because of a series of unplanned events: a snowfall which means she cannot leave Kelso; a folk event at the local pub the same night she is in town; a wrong turn that forces her to lose her way in the streets of the town – all of which distract her from her singular aim of collecting tales. Prudencia gets lost, in more than one sense, leading to a significant shift in her self-awareness, and a stumbling and unsettling discovery of her own tale. Through this experience, she learns that in order to fully *be,* to participate in life, she cannot always be an observer: the moral of this tale is one it shares with *The Twisted Heart*. *The Strange Undoing* also presents us with a lesson about research: that to take an overly rational and orderly approach to a subject like folk tales is to miss the point; rather, one should allow for the possibility of encounters with the strange and wonderful.

The idea that a collection *should be* exhaustive, ordered, and based on a particular principle is a Western idea about knowledge inherited from the Enlightenment. Shifts in ideas about research and knowledge from the late eighteenth and early nineteenth centuries contributed not only to significant changes in universities, facilitating the advent of the PhD as a *research* degree, but also the establishment and renovation of libraries and museums that replaced the individualistic collections or *Wunderkammer* of old. Clark (2006) writes that transformations in the *collection* of books, or the emergence of the modern research library, were bound up with transformations in the *interrelation* of books, the system of knowledge. The emergence of the modern library thus correlates to a shift in the idea of academic knowledge from erudition, as Clark puts it, to research during the Enlightenment. Other collections also began to be organised according to complex systems, rather than on the basis of an individual collector's interest. As Daston and Park (2001) suggest, mystery and the fantastic were uncoupled from curiosity during the Enlightenment, and wonder in the strange ceased to be the organising principle for collections. As part of this move away from the fantastic, the metaphysical university declined, engendered by a loss of *mystery*, as Barnett (2011) describes, and a decreased interest in exploring beyond that which exists in the knowable world.

The Strange Undoing speaks to, and disrupts, a distinction between collection as an openness to mystery and the strange, and collection as the orderly, systematic assemblage and organisation of something. To do this it follows, as described above, what is becoming a familiar narrative form for tales about doctoral research (see Kostova, 2005; Goodman, 2010; Harkness, 2011), in which the researchers embark on a project armed with tools of observation, orderly methods of data collection, and rationality. In the course of doing the research, they become somewhat obsessive about their task, seeking to uncover more, and more unusual or hitherto unknown finds. Through encounters with increasingly 'strange facts' (Daston and Park, 2001), they gradually (or sometimes suddenly) must acknowledge the seemingly impossible – for example, the existence of the Devil, or of Dracula. Further, through the process of seeking the unusual, desire (to know, to have) is unlocked, and the rationality that once governed their approach to research is replaced by something far less controlled. As stories like this tell us, desire has no limits (Harkness, 2011). Prudencia's desire to collect, catalogue and *know* Border folk turns into an obsession that is dangerous, at least to herself. Prudencia, whose very name connotes prudence, becomes less the rational and restrained being that she tries to be, and which is the PhD Enlightenment ideal (Johnson *et al.*, 2000), and tips her towards being the kind of unhinged collector-figure she knows from her own childhood, and fears becoming.

One could argue that a collector's desire has no limits because collections are always, potentially, inexhaustible. Parameters are set or determined, their end-points constructed. In the play, none of the collections *are* complete, because no-one can know the totality of Border folk, past and present, or of souls in the world, or of books written and unwritten. Omissions are inevitable; the desire of the collector-researcher cannot be completely satisfied. Allegra Goodman's novel *The Cookbook Collector* (2010), tells a similar tale. George, who did a PhD in thermal dynamics then made his money in Microsoft, has no interest in pursuing a career in academia, yet loves finding rare books, so, after relinquishing both academia and Silicon Valley, he buys a bookshop in Berkeley. Like Prudencia's father, George hankers after objects from a pre-digital era, *tangible things*, including the rare cookbooks he discovers, and which he employs graduate student Jess to catalogue. George's desire for rare things is tinged with a kind of despair: he 'hungers' for beautiful and authentic *things* yet, once obtained, these only temporarily sate his longing, which never abates, has no end, because there are always more things to be sought and found.

The hankering after tangibles that George experiences highlights an aspect of research that a doctoral project which reimagines doctoral research also underscores. NZ artist Tessa Laird's installation of clay books, first exhibited as *Reading Room* (2012) and then as *Chupacabra Candelabra* (2013, 2014),[1] is a recreation of her bibliography for her doctorate in Fine Arts. The books represent three years of research reading. Originally, in *Reading Room*, the books were individually sculpted. According to art critic Were (2013), these unopenable books mock the fetishizing of books as objects by collectors who have little interest in their content. The simple clay structures also have a folk dimension: they are handmade of earthy materials and suggest a cottage industry, evoking an era that predates mass production (Were, 2013: 74), like George's cookbooks and records in Goodman's novel. Another art critic points to associations between species of birds that have been hunted to extinction – partly in the name of collection, partly for science – and the book or paperback now also under threat of extinction in the digital age (Dunn, 2012; Were, 2013). Rare and extinct things are favoured objects for collections, which also enable their preservation.

At one level, Laird's installation makes tangible the reading list for her doctorate, and so points to the means by which *every* doctoral research project involves collection. It is a fundament of doctoral research to undertake a systematic review of the literature, and to demonstrate in the thesis, via the bibliography or list of references or works cited, the texts that have been read and cited. Every thesis contains its own particular collection, which is ordered as a system based on particular principles. Laird's collection is therefore not only a reading list for a particular doctoral thesis made tangible, it is also a reminder of the 'collection' in every doctoral thesis *and* a comment on way in which knowledge and collections of books are interrelated. As Clark (2006) reminds, the Enlightenment transformation in the collection and interrelation of books, that is, the system of knowledge, is bound up with a shift *to* research.

The exhibition of clay books highlights one further aspect of research that is also present in *The Strange Undoing*: the capacity of an encounter with an 'other' kind of knowledge that sits outside the Western Enlightenment frame. In *Chupacabra Candelabra*, the books are stacked to form towers, topped with candelabra-like shapes, recalling mystical objects from different religions: Hindu statues of multi-limbed goddesses and Jewish *memorahs*. By representing her doctoral reading list in this way, Laird not only shows, as a good doctoral scholar, that she has read widely, drawing on both academic literature and mystical literature; she also reveals an openness to *other* knowledges, and other kinds of encounters.

Research wonder: strange encounters

If *The Strange Undoing of Prudencia Hart* cautions against over-reliance on rationality, it also advances the case for *chance encounters* in research. Prudencia's carefully planned research trip goes astray with the advent of the snowstorm, allowing her to experience the strange and unsettling tale in a way that her scholarly approach to folk had hitherto inhibited. Writing about qualitative research, MacLure (2013) argues that a counterpoint to the exercise of reason in approaching data is *more wonder*. Wonder, she argues, arises both from an interpretative stance, in the form of an openness to not knowing, and to data collection. The possibilities for wonder in research are created by asides in interviews, or fragments of field notes – moments that 'confound' a more mechanical search for meanings or patterns, but also engender further thought. Significantly, moments like these tend to arise from data not planned for, or anticipated, in the design of the research, occurring instead when we do not set out to 'collect' them (MacLure, 2013). This recalls Prudencia's story and also the historians of Kostova's novel, whose planned doctoral projects are suspended by their diversion into researching Dracula – a research side alley which in their case leads to an encounter with the uncanny, and which has profound consequences.

A state of wonder can also be induced by encounters *with* wonders, things that exceed, or bring into question, the known. According to Daston and Park (2001), for seventeenth-century-thinkers, wonders acted as an impetus for inquiry. Wonders sat at the limits or edges of the known, signalling the unknown and acting as a spur to further research and investigation. Since the Enlightenment, they argue, wonder has become somewhat disreputable in 'workaday sciences', smacking of amateur or childish pursuits, evocative of fantasy and folk tale no longer considered scientific. This is partly because the state of wonder, like desire, is one in which the rational self is not in command. MacLure (2013) describes it as a threshold experience in which one is suspended between knowing and unknowing, and is therefore not safe. The price one pays for wonder, she continues, is the ruin of certainty. MacLure, like Daston and Park (2001), refers to the cabinets of curiosities or *Wunderkammer* of the sixteenth through to the eighteenth centuries, collections made on the cusp of modernity and scientific rationality, yet which held something of the allure of miracles and magic that belonged to an earlier world. Cabinets of curiosities have become something of a synecdoche for pre-Enlightenment knowledge.

Collections based on principles that are unknown, seem random, or contain wonders also evoke encounters with forms of knowledge organised by non-Western epistemology, like Borges' Chinese encyclopaedia, referred to in the preface to Michel Foucault's *The Order of Things* (1994/1970), in which the encounter with an 'other' order of things, another system, engenders a shake-up to epistemic certainty, calling into question the known order as given or universal. Laird is gesturing to this kind of shake-up with her collection of books and mystical objects in *Chupacabra Candelabra*. The representations of research I have analysed in literary and popular culture signal the *limits* of knowledge, even, in some cases, to the unknowable, or ineffable. Emerging is an emphasis in contemporary representations of research which connects a recognition of the limits of *language* (such as the linguistic turn has engendered), with a recognition of the limits of traditional Western Enlightenment *knowledge*. Two significant lines of thought can be identified in relation to the latter. The first acknowledges what non-Western knowledge traditions, including Eastern mystical traditions (Zembylas and Michaelides, 2004; Sousanis, 2014), or knowledge that could be termed Southern theory (Connell, 2007; Manathunga, 2014) reveal about the limits of Western knowledge.

The second line of enquiry forces an acknowledgement of how *matter* adds to, or differently frames, our understanding of research, as highlighted by new materialism. After all, it is an encounter with random objects or *things* that is the catalyst for Jane Bennett (2010) to consider the possibility that matter can be 'vital' in ways that exceed human understanding. Bennett highlights that our tendency to explain things in terms of accepted ways of knowing inhibits our capacity to see or understand objects in anything other than anthropomorphic terms. Yet *things* can have a power of their own, she suggests, requiring moments of methodological naïveté for us to apprehend them. The question, she writes, is how do we attain (or perhaps *retain*) this kind of naiveté? One possibility is to allow ourselves to be 'infected' by ideas or philosophies that have been discredited, or to be tainted by pre-modern attitudes of superstition, animism and the like (Bennett, 2010).

Something like this kind of epistemological shake-up happens to the doctoral researcher (and to some extent the reader) in China Mieville's *The City and the City* (2009). The world of this novel, a work of fantasy fiction, is like and unlike ours, recognisable yet utterly other (in fantasy and science fiction circles this is 'worlding'). At the start of this novel, the body of a young American PhD student in archaeology, Mahalia Geary, is found in the city of Besźel. Besźel, we learn, is 'crosshatched' with another city Ul Qoma. The two cities belong to different countries, are separately administered, and the residents of each have developed the ability to not acknowledge each other. The cities do not interact, even though they (physically) intersect. They are simultaneously present and absent in each other's reality, presence/absence being one of the many binary oppositions the novel calls into question.

As she was a resident of Ul Qoma, Mahalia's body should not be in Besźel at all and the fact that it is leads to a high-level investigation. In order to find out more about Mahalia's research, and what it has to do with her death, Inspector Borlù travels to the other city to talk to her supervisor, Professor Isabelle Nancy, a Canadian academic working on the archaeological dig of Bol Ye'an in Ul Quoma. As Borlù soon discovers, Mahalia's research was into the early history of the area and the origins of the two cities: she was interested in theories that the different cities shared a common ancient historical source before they split, an event referred to (although not universally accepted as fact) as Cleavage. As her supervisor terms it, the archaeological research team at the Bol Ye'an site is uncovering artefacts millennia old: 'root stuff'. The objects found at Bol Ye'an are legendary, inside and outside academic circles, and although Professor Nancy does not acknowledge their supposed magic powers, she does allow that as a material culture it *makes no sense*. Items that should have been located in distant epochs were instead contemporaneous – the objects disallowed stratigraphy, so the researchers involved had to stop trying to identify or follow a particular sequence and 'just look.' The objects found in the dig at Bol Ye'an are a collection of things which calls into question firmly held and long-accepted ideas of periodicity and the linearity of time.

In addition to her work with the objects found in the dig, Mahalia was interested in the theory that the two cities share not only a single origin, but are still linked by Orciny, a legendary third city that secretly rules the other two via a kind of illuminati. Like many (rational) others, Borlù considers the legends of Orciny to be the stuff of rumour and legend, old wives' tales and urban myths. It turns out that the PhD student Mahalia was obsessed with legends of Orciny: she was a folklorist, into the old stories now seldom told, even to children, like Prudencia. This strand of her research was secret; while she pursued her doctoral research in archaeology, Mahalia also researched the esoteric and mysterious Orciny, although according to her supervisor, the doctoral project itself had nothing to do with the legends of Orciny which, while a legitimate topic for a PhD in folklore, anthropology or comparative literature, was not 'real' archaeology, which is working with actual *object*s, not stories. The supervisor admits to Borlù that she felt some disappointment with Mahalia's doctoral writing, which, despite her obvious intelligence and long work hours, was fairly ordinary and slight, as if Mahalia's real interest lay with the secret research she was doing into the 'ur-myth' of Orciny, rather than her legitimate empirical doctoral work (Mieville, 2009).

The division between Mahalia's doctoral research, approved by her supervisor, and her secret, fringe research into Orciny, can be read as a comment on what is currently valued as legitimate research in universities, of which Miéville, who has a PhD from the London School of Economics, and has worked as an academic, has first-hand knowledge. As Barnett (2011) suggests, opportunities to experience wonder and mystery, for making 'strange connections' across kinds of knowledge, or experiencing leaps of the imagination, are not encouraged in the contemporary university. He goes on to detail the ways in which the current research university *limits thought*, in contrast to its forebear, the metaphysical university:

> The research university ... is an institution for closing thought and understanding rather than opening thought. The proposition will seem heretical to many. But, to repeat, we only have to notice that many categories relating to thought and understanding are now – except in fringe activities – outlawed on campus: the sacred, the sublime, wonder, mystery, awe, wisdom, oneness and spirit.
>
> (Barnett, 2011: 26)

These elements, Barnett argues, are not only devalued, they are also currently seen as dangerous, and are therefore de-legitimated. The rare possibility for 'unbridled leaps' that the current discourse allows is in terms of innovation and creativity, usually limited to the technological.

Nonetheless, the sacred, sublime, wonder and mystery *are* still associated with the university in cultural practices, appearing in representations of research in literature and popular culture. This indicates a deep social imaginary of the kind that Taylor (2004) identifies, and which surfaces in contemporary representations. Wizardry, arcane knowledge and formal education are sometimes closely aligned in popular culture – as the *Harry Potter* novels attest. Elements of the old transcendentalism of the university remain, as Clark (2006) suggests, even though the university ostensibly lost this aspect of its mission after the Enlightenment. It is in ideas like academic charisma that we find a counterpoint to rationalism and disenchantment, for example. He also makes the point that scientists in popular culture (such as the proliferation of shows depicting forensic science on television, including *Bones*) are today's wizards – that scientific knowledge is akin to the power of magic.

While there is perhaps a tendency to depict encounters with wonder and mystery as occurring for researchers in disciplines like history, folklore or cultural studies, as in *The Strange Undoing of Prudencia Hart* or *The City and the City*, representations of research in the sciences are not excluded from this association. The geophysicists in Kim Stanley Robinson's late twentieth-century novel *Antarctica* (1997), or mathematicians in the film *Proof* (2005), demonstrate this. In these texts, encounters with wonder, awe and the sublime are reasons for conducting research, or occur as a result of a research encounter with a seeming empirical anomaly – what Daston and Park (2001) term a 'strange fact'. A strange fact might be something detected through methods of empirical science (like careful observation), yet which does not fit with known laws. Some strange facts can disturb known orders – such as our understanding of time. This is the issue that Mahalia's supervisor is grappling with on the archaeological dig: the evidence tells her that time as she understands it needs to be reconsidered. In Robinson's *Antarctica* (1997), the encounter with an anomaly forces the researchers to adopt a different interpretative frame from the dominant one, creating an epistemological schism in the field of research.

A *danger* of wonder is that it may not lead to inquiry, but instead inhibit it. Schmitt and Lahroodi (2008) have argued that curiosity, rather than wonder, is a preferable attribute in a university student. If wonder arises from a mystery, for example, it is not accompanied by the need to solve the mystery – unlike curiosity, which motivates inquiry (Schmitt and Lahroodi, 2008: 132). Taking a similar view, that wonder transfixes rather than spurs to action, yet differing in her perception of its value, Bennett (2001) argues that not only is disenchantment overemphasised in modern life, but that wonder and a capacity for enchantment in contemporary times needs to be recognised as occurring, and more widely celebrated. According to Bennett, enchantment or a state of wonder *is* to be transfixed or spellbound and it involves being 'carried away', present and yet not present. Bronwyn Lloyd (PhD, Art History), describes this research state in her written imagining, which is in her case induced by an encounter in an archive, as the experience of being in a second location, here and yet not here (see also Lloyd, 2011).

Being transfixed by wonder or enchantment may court danger, but it can also be conducive to learning, in that it is transformative for the individual. As nineteenth-century writer and theorist John Ruskin argued, experiencing fathomless mystery is important *to* learning and growing as an individual. This is a fairly familiar narrative trajectory in fiction, in particular fantasy or science fiction, in which an individual – often a researcher – encounters something seemingly entirely *other* and is at first transfixed, and then transformed by it. For the researchers in Robinson's *Antarctica*, the encounter with an anomaly, in a landscape that itself induces wonder, works like this, and not only is it personally transformative for the researchers, but it is also a goad to inquiry and further research that questions the very assumptions of the field.

There are times, however, in stories about doctoral research, where the opposite happens, and an encounter with wonder or the uncanny engenders a personal transformation on the part of the researcher that eclipses the research, which is then completed in a cursory way, or simply abandoned. This occurs in *The Historian*: the completion of their doctoral research projects is less of a priority for Helen and Paul after their encounters with Dracula (and why not!). There are also tales of defection, as with stories I discuss in the following chapter, where doctoral researchers encounter something unexpected which leads to a radical transformation of another kind, and they do not emerge to rejoin academic society. The frequency with which this story is told and retold intimates that mystery and wonder are *part of* a deeply held cultural imaginary of research. If so, the potential for disruptive encounters engendered by research is always present.

Research writing

The transformative potential of encounters with knowledge are particularly apparent in stories of the PhD in which writing the thesis is the focus. In the twenty-first-century imaginary writing the thesis is conceptualised in two related ways: it is bound up with *coming to know* for the individual doctoral student-subject, and it is the means of making an original contribution to knowledge in broader terms. As writing is so central to how doctoral research is imagined and constructed in discourse, the thesis writing process gives insight into how *knowledge* is produced. The close association of writing with knowledge dates from the PhD's conception: as underscored by Clark (2006), the research university came into being in Europe as writing gained ascendency over orality, and as other kinds of knowledge were squeezed out. Writing is the close companion of reason and empirical knowledge, and is therefore firmly part of our imaginary of the research university. Just think of Carlyle's association of the 'true university' with a 'collection of books' and a 'man of letters'. Despite changes to universities over the last 200 years, *writing* is still central to our idea of the university.

It is perhaps the case, however, that the nature of writing (Carlyle's 'letters') in the current university context (putting aside for a moment the issue of 'man') *has* changed. Would we still claim that a measure of a university is its collection of books? Others have considered the issue of 'the book' and its relationship to the contemporary university (Readings, 1996; Brew, 2001; Collini, 2012; Rolfe, 2013; Barnett, 2015;) but there is scant consideration of what the decline of the book (if such a thing is happening) might mean for the PhD thesis, which is, after all, a book. There are of course other forms of research output (to use the contemporary parlance) for different kinds of doctorates, which occasionally gives rise to calls for a different kind of PhD (Park, 2007). There are also shifts in notions of what scholarship *is*, as ideas about, and practices associated with, academic time change, which may yet give rise to greater change (Barnett, 2015). As yet there is, nonetheless, a degree of stability in *this*: the PhD continues to have as its central measure a written thesis. It is still, to echo Derrida (2004), the time of the thesis.

Presently, writing a thesis is a familiar, possibly over-determined, imaginary in doctoral education literature. Writing about doctoral writing has proliferated in recent times. Research into thesis-writing and writing for publication is a significant strand of contemporary scholarship in this field (Aitchison, *et al*., 2010; Thomson and Kamler, 2013), there are numerous informative guide-books on how to write a thesis (Dunleavy, 2003; Wisker, 2007; Carter *et al*., 2012) and the online presence of blogs on doctoral writing offering writing support and advice (DoctoralWriting SIG, patter, The Thesis Whisperer) is strong. It is not unusual across these forums for writing to be treated as a difficulty to be overcome (Owler, 2010). In the cluster of guides and how-to books on thesis writing are works that, although containing many useful tips for writers, make fairly light of 'the writing process', and share with institutions the perception that self-management is the key to productive (busy) writing and will result in thesis completion. While the *difficulty* of writing may be recognised, it is often in terms of a problem – one that leads to long completion times, or (worse), attrition. As this suggests, a prevalent view of thesis writing is that it is *a risk to be managed* (Owler, 2010; Barnacle and Dall'Alba, 2013).

In the current higher education era, writing is bound up with performativity, for an individual (usually measured in terms of publication) and for the institution – the number of PhD theses, completed theses that is, is taken into account in a research institution's performance. In NZ, for example, completed PhDs are accounted for in the six-yearly research assessment exercise, the Performance Based Research Fund (PBRF). This can put pressure on institutions, as well as doctoral researchers and their supervisors, but that is not the only issue. As Barnett (2015) has recently argued, academic work is institutionalised work and the brisk pace at which institutions currently operate influences the nature of the work. Expectations shift as *time* factors into both how knowledge claims are formed, and how they are assessed (Barnett, 2015). Time – in particular time to completion – is likewise more than ever a significant element of thesis writing. As writing about thesis-writing occurs in this context, it is bound up with the trend to make the PhD, like other aspects of academic work, both less risky and more efficient.

A benefit arising from scrutiny of doctoral thesis-writing is that writing is recognised as *work* involving practical considerations, labour and hard graft. On the other hand, an emphasis on the practical dimensions can underplay the pleasure or passion of writing, or the significant identity shifts that arise from working on doctorate, all of which are less easy to account for. Notable exceptions in current literature on writing a doctorate acknowledge the complexity of writing for research purposes, recognising that it is bound up with identity formation, or with emotion and affect (Burford, 2015), and with ideas and imaginaries about being a researcher, or a scholar. Thomson and Kamler's (2013) book on writing for publication, aimed at doctoral candidates or recent graduates, devotes the first chapter to the writer, outlining the ways in which writing is entwined with taking up an identity of a scholar, one that owes its lineage to ideas of monastic scholarship.

This particular imaginary, of the scholar working quietly and alone on a thesis, with time to do so, is still live in twenty-first-century imaginaries of doctoral research. It is captured by one of the participants in my study, PhD graduate Isabel Haarhaus (English literature), who describes writing her PhD thesis as 'privileged extended deep thinking time; time to think without financial pressure'. When prompted to consider if her imagined PhD was similar to her lived experience, she wrote in her *petits recits* that it was, 'insofar as I imagined it as a solitary exploration and production':

> I imagined myself sitting at a desk, alone, under a lamp, surrounded by books, papers, notes and resources, thinking and writing and thinking some more; and that is exactly how it was . . . It was the space and the time and the clear focus on thinking and writing that allowed my imagination to flourish. I have never thought so deeply again or sustained such a complex train or tree of thought or dwelt so intensely on texts and ideas or written so much as when I did my Doctorate.

Isabel's imagined and remembered space is, as she terms it, the 'classic scholar's image' of a 'monastic' space in which the individual is 'cloistered away from the world, in a small bespoke place for contemplation'. She draws on a long-held and traditional idea in Western and Eastern cultures of the scholar as a solitary figure in a room: Chinese folk tales include many depictions of solitary scholars, for instance. Like the scholars of legend, the imagined research space that Isabel describes is one which enables deep, complex thought, and produces the kind of knowledge, like a Chinese scholar's secrets of life, that are *only* accessible when alone. Isabel's images of doctoral research are all of 'a solitary figure in a cosy space. Quiet and dimly lit. Closed off to the world and its demands.' It resembles the space that Bachelard (1994/1958) imagines for his hermit in the sense that it is removed from worldly demands, and is a space of reverie and contemplation.

At the same time, the cloistered nature of the space that Isabel actually inhabited while doing her PhD was carefully contrived. As a mother of a small child, Isabel *made* the space and the time for her PhD:

> I used to close all the blinds and work under a lamp. My desk was my great-grandfather's desk and it was in my new son's room. I had photographs of important people and tidied it up each day. I left notes to myself as to where I was up to so as not to lose a moment of thinking and writing time the next time I sat down at my desk. I was highly organised, partly because I had a baby and time was precious . . . When I finished, tidied away my papers, turned off the light and opened the blind, it was as if I had emerged from a trance.

One of the techniques Isabel used to distinguish and demarcate the research time (a specific three hours per day) and space (the desk in her son's room) was to turn on and off her lamp: the light signalled the beginning and end of writing time. Bachelard writes that the image of the lamp is a significant and recurring image in the poetics of space: the lamp is not lit out of doors, but is enclosed. As it appears at a window to an outside spectator, it represents the warmth and protected (and excluding) nature of the space inside; it can also signify that someone is working, bent over a desk, dogged and solitary (1994/1958). When Bachelard describes a solitary figure enclosed in light, he emphasises the labour he or she undertakes; reverie for Bachelard is not dreamy posturing; rather it is the activity that produces thought.

Similarly, Isabel clearly constructs writing as *work*. The verbs she uses in her written imagining convey the nature of the research that she does in this (determined) space. The effect of this is that even as she presents us with a somewhat idealised view of a scholarly haven, she also brings this image back from the brink of romanticism by underscoring that research is *labour*, a term that she uses several times. The figure in the imagined 'cosy space' is not dreamily chewing a pencil but is 'concentrating, straining, delving, thinking, solving, exploring, experimenting'. In her written account of a PhD imaginary, Isabel celebrates this aspect of research and likens the doctoral researcher to anyone intent on his or her work, not only a 'writer writing', but also 'a sculptor sculpting, a baker baking, a musician playing, a carpenter building'. Later, she takes the analogy with manual work further and writes of the editing stage of producing a thesis as 'similar to working in a really hot orchard; it was row by row, block by block, and it was hard labour', often requiring her to get on 'all fours, editing', which she sometimes did in her underwear 'because it was so hot!'

The material and economic conditions that enabled Isabel to work are also acknowledged: she needed not only the money from her scholarship but also the legitimacy that it afforded in order to do it – to know that her time was not a waste, that her *research* labour was valued. There are echoes of Virginia Woolf (1989/1929) in Isabel's construction of 'a room of one's own', and in her engagement with the idea of Woolf's famous polemic that at base, economic independence is critical for enabling work. As Isabel writes, 'For me it really comes down to the conditions of production: having the time, the money and the legitimacy to think and write, and to be accorded status while doing so.'

In addition, again echoing Woolf, a sense of tradition and knowledge of forebears (it is her great-grandfather's desk she writes at), is important to Isabel. Like Woolf, she searches through history looking for predecessors – other women who write. To convey this tradition of women working in a space they had managed to carve out, or create from the demands of the rest of their life, Isabel constructed a mosaic of images of solitary women working in a 'cosy space'. And so, although she draws on an imaginary of a scholar that evokes a male scholarly tradition, Carlyle's 'man of letters', she primarily imagines *women* in this space:

> I was very much alone, and blissfully so. I felt part of a long tradition of women who had managed to find a 'room of one's own', if only for a brief moment in time, to create something other than children and meals or do women's work, like teaching other forms of service. It was important to me that I was paid to do it, as this legitimised the time and the effort. I was at my happiest at my desk with my thoughts and my work. I used to close all the blinds and work under a lamp.

This final phrase again echoes Woolf: 'It would be better to draw the curtains; to shut out distractions; to light the lamp' (1989/1929: 47). For Isabel, however, even the distractions were less *that* than a healthy counterpoint to the solitary and (what could be seen as) cerebral acts of thinking and writing. She writes that when she turned out the light, opened the blinds and emerged from the trance, she returned to the work of being a mother:

> Then I would carry on with wonderfully different, down-to-earth duties: feeding my son, tending to his body, preparing the dinner, washing the nappies etc. It was a perfect balanced combination for me: the cloistered esoteric private space of the thinking and writing, then the bodily, social, public life of being a mother of a small child.

Age-old binaries of public and private, body and mind, are engaged with in this account of research, but here they are balanced, enabling this PhD researcher to extract pleasure from both, undermining the traditional gendering of each. This pleasure is further emphasised by the way that Isabel writes of the tasks that she engages in: both the research work and the work of being a mother are, while in some ways mundane, nonetheless invested with joy of a deep and satisfying kind. Even though the editing was hard, grunt-work, and made more so by the fact that by this stage she was heavily pregnant with her second child, Isabel writes that it was nonetheless 'also magnificent in terms of the depth of thinking, the rigor of the work'. Interestingly, a similar idea is established in Kirsty Gunn's (2012) novel *The Big Music* in which the narrator – Helen, who did a PhD at Glasgow – intersperses writing (which is adamantly *working*) with maternal and filial love and care. Writing is part of a *life*. I am also reminded of Bachelard's (1994/1958) question regarding how housework could be made into a creative activity, possible through integrating reverie into work, by investing ordinary objects or tasks with the imagination. Isabel's research tasks and domestic tasks are labour, but they are also more than that, because she is able to draw on an imaginary of scholars and writers, in particular women, inhabiting similar spaces. Because the research tasks are undertaken in a space which is created by Isabel, enabled by her economic status (*à la* Woolf), she is then able to truly inhabit the space, and take pleasure in the work.

Not all accounts of doctoral writing reflect on the joy. In many stories about writing, it is cast as overwhelmingly difficult. In recent fiction, writing the thesis is usually a torturous process that goes in fits and starts, meanders, occasionally stops altogether (see Niffenegger, 2009; Maltman, 2012). Only some doctoral candidates complete. Thesis writer Rosemary Summers in *Magpie Hall*, by NZ writer Rachael King (2009), experiences writing in this way. For Rosemary, writing is difficult partly because it is entwined with *other things* – love and desire and grief. Rosemary's completion of her thesis depends upon her accessing *and* overcoming past trauma and guilt that is both personal, and cultural. Rosemary's own narrative, set in the twenty-first century, entwines with a narrative set in the nineteenth-century colonial past. In the contemporary narrative, Rosemary is a research student writing her 'interminable' thesis on Victorian literature. Her thesis topic is romantic love in Victorian Gothic novels, which gives an indication of the kind of literature that not only informs Rosemary's views of romantic love and gender roles, but also forms the basis of the novel's own textual influences. At the start of the novel, Rosemary leaves the university to escape a complicated relationship with her supervisor and lover Hugh, and heads to her rural ancestral home, built in the nineteenth century. She takes her thesis with her in the car, intending to spend quiet uninterrupted time writing, although her thesis has become something of a burden.

Rosemary is not the only student to characterise her thesis in this way. It is partly because there is so much at stake that doctoral writing is conceptualised as a burden which cannot be cast off, or as a fraught activity: the PhD is awarded primarily on the basis of the written thesis. Yet current practices, including how-to books and institutional workshops on writing, can arguably be seen to increase anxiety about writing, rather than ameliorate it, because they are removed from actual writing experiences, which, as pointed out by Barnacle and Dall'Alba (2013), are less smooth than the representations denote. These authors make the claim that thesis writing is currently understood primarily in terms of mastery and control, as conceptualised by Heidegger: *they* aim to engage with the 'joy and risk' of writing, and with the instability of meaning (Barnacle and Dall'Alba, 2013). What Barnacle and Dall'Alba intimate is that *anxiety and risk* are not only part of writing, but are a productive component. In other words, they are not a problem to be managed or overcome, but a necessary dimension of doctoral research, which *is* difficult and involves producing original knowledge. Furthermore, knowledge in these terms is not simply a contribution in the form of a thesis, a commodity, something that can be possessed by the individual doctoral candidate, or offered to the university; rather, it is enacted and lived by the doctoral subject – it is a way of *being* (Barnacle and Dall'Alba, 2013).

Although Rosemary embraces a different way of being by the end of the novel, in that she *becomes a writer*, it is not an easy transition. That Rosemary feels the need to leave the university in order to write (not an uncommon trope in stories about thesis-writing) reflects the extent to which writing is impacted upon by the context in which it happens – the place, in this case, of the suffocating English department (see also Byatt, 2000; Collins, 2006) and the relationships she has with those around her, in particular her supervisor, which Chapter 3 returns to. Rosemary's idea of being holed up in the old house writing is both familiar, echoing Bachelard (1994) for instance, and something of a fantasy: the idea that with uninterrupted time and space she will finally be able to finish. Another similar fantasy has already been abandoned – one where she and Hugh would live in Wales in a cottage in the hills and finish their respective projects. In Sarah Moss' novel *Night Waking* (2012), post-doctoral researcher Anna and her academic husband do precisely this, and take themselves off to a remote Scottish island, so that she can finish her book, and he can observe the local puffin population. Predictably, it does not go smoothly, partly as they struggle to balance work with caring for their two young children in a remote setting. Relationships, not to mention economic factors, are seldom as easily put aside for writing and research as we sometimes imagine (see also Maltman, 2012).

The idea that writing happens *away* from the world in some kind of vacuum of pure ideas, without others' input, distraction, or the hassle of economic concerns, draws on an imaginary of writing as springing from the mind of the individual genius, a Romantic conception contemporaneous with the 'hero of knowledge' that Clark (2006) describes. Thomson and Kamler argue *against* this idea and consider that it is important research writers avoid lapsing into notions of creativity and imagination springing from the individual who is somehow outside of a social context. Writing is not an individual practice, they argue, that happens in a 'lonely garret'; rather, it is always socially situated (Thomson and Kamler, 2013). The myth of the writer in the garret that Rosemary invokes (and she does spend a fair bit of time in the attic of the old house) overlooks two important related factors about writing: that it is, as Thomson and Kamler argue, socially situated, and that it is work in the way that Isabel constructs it. To take the first point, writing is *for* someone to read, it involves the reader (including thesis examiners) and so it is always dialogic (Bakhtin, 1998¹). Writing is also drafting, rewriting, rewriting, editing, preferably *with* input from others, including supervisors, peers, colleagues and even finally the examiners.

In *Magpie Hall*, Rosemary is at first held in stasis: she is as unable to write in the old house as she was in the university. Feeling behind schedule is a sensation Rosemary shares with other thesis writers, real and imagined (Byatt, 2000; Niffenegger, 2009; Gowers, 2009), as is the determination to begin in earnest, followed usually by a self-sabotaging distraction, which happens more than once. Her energy and dissipation for writing the thesis go in cycles. Owler (2010) refers to this trope (often comedic, as in Jorge Cham's *PhD* comic strip) as familiar in the literature that aims to promote self-management of the writing process and to improve the self-sabotaging behaviours of committing to other activities, procrastination or even perfectionism (Kearns, 2008; Owler, 2010).

Against this idea, Owler posits another conceptualisation, drawing on the work of Maurice Blanchot, who is in turn drawing on Heidegger's ideas about the relationship of being to knowledge. According to this account, the doctoral writers begin in the dark, working in the productive realm of uncertainty with a question that impels them forward, seeking answers, or truth. Writing involves oscillating between confusion and clarity, and doctoral writers swing between excitement, as they find answers, and anxiety or uncertainty, as their initial question takes new and different forms. This idea captures something of the perpetual movement or oscillation for the researcher – between rationality and desire, between the known (or knowable) and the strange – that is constructed over and over in twenty-first-century stories about doctoral research.

Endnote

1 *Chupacabra Candelabra* was first exhibited at Melanie Roger Gallery, Auckland, 2013; then as part of the Auckland City Art Gallery *Freedom Farmers* exhibition 2013–2014, curated by Natasha Conland.

CHAPTER 2

The idea of the PhD researcher

> Even as his heart was breaking, a stream of words was coming out of his mouth that he felt no identification with or control over whatsoever. 'Consultancy,' 'core competencies,' 'client relationship,' 'maintain ownership of the process.' It was like a robot talking. He, or it, talked faster and faster, trying to stay ahead of his own feelings of shame and doubt, which loomed over him like a breaking wave curling above a surfer.
>
> (Grossman, 2012: 325)

> Who needs another person with a doctorate in something or other?
> (Trapido, 2012: 25)

According to an idea of the PhD in the mid twentieth century, doctoral scholars were intending academics, with an academic position the assumed end goal. A PhD thesis was *a life's work*, both in the sense of taking a substantial chunk of a lifespan to complete, and in terms of what the scholar contributed to the discipline, therefore defining him or her as an academic. This kind of academic person-formation occurred not just *in* the discipline but in a specific, narrow area of research: producing a Shakespearean scholar, for instance, rather than scholar of English literature. And it was primarily within this fairly narrow context that an individual doctoral scholar came to assume an academic identity.

At least, that is how I think the story went. For the field of representation was also different in the twentieth century: written accounts about becoming a PhD were not common, and were mainly found in biographies and memoirs of academic life (Reimer, 1998). Inside the academy, before everything went online, if a PhD statute existed few people ever saw it, and institutional lists of graduate attributes have only become a phenomenon since the 1990s (Bosanquet *et al.*, 2012). There *were* ideas about what a PhD was, of course, but their articulations in textual form were thinner on the ground; I would have been hard pressed to find enough data for this book. The PhD candidate was thus a less defined, more shadowy figure, rarely glimpsed in discursive form.

Of course in real terms there were also fewer actual PhD bodies than there are now, those that there *were*, were fairly homogenous. Since the late twentieth century, interest in and scrutiny of the PhD has increased exponentially with greater numbers of actual doctoral enrolments. In addition, possibly as a result, there is a plethora of discursive constructions of the PhD student. As the field of doctoral education has grown into its own area of research, articulations of what a PhD *is* or is meant to be – or could be – are ever increasing. In this field, two strands seemed to dominate research into doctoral education around the turn of the twenty-first century: a focus on the PhD as a contribution to knowledge, usually in the form of a research project, and a focus on the development of the candidate, a skilled researcher (Park, 2007). (A third related strand was supervision.) This perceived dual aspect of the PhD 'outcome' was captured by the pithy and reductive catchphrase *person vs. product*.

Arguably, the doctoral student-subject is not now simply the intending or hopeful academic. In research literature, doctoral education is considered not only for its role in contributing to a process of academic identity-formation (McAlpine and Lucas, 2011), but also in terms of producing other kinds of knowledge workers (Tennant, 2005). Yet somehow, rather than providing new conceptions of the Doctor of Philosophy, or other possibilities for post-doctoral identities, ideas about the PhD in the broader discursive domain and popular culture reinscribe aspects of a more traditional figure of the academic, or scholar. Elements of this figure are at odds with the outcomes for doctoral graduates emphasized in institutional discourse and national and transnational descriptors, which conceptualise doctoral graduates as skilled workers fit for a globalised KE.

This idea of a skilled knowledge worker is currently the ideal or 'good' doctoral student, and is my initial focus in this chapter. What are the desirable attributes of this particular doctoral identity? Luckily (or unluckily, depending on your perspective), there is a wealth of literature outlining what these are. Some describe an individual suited both to contemporary academia in a neoliberal era *and* to research in non-academic domains, with skills such as self-development, flexibility and the capacity to be mobile and adaptable, and having advanced technological ability and a range of interpersonal and communication skills. At the same time, traditional doctoral characteristics such as reason and independence are also articulated as desirable in PhD graduates. We are witnessing an amalgamation of the Enlightenment figure of the PhD hero of knowledge (Clark, 2006) with the good subject of and for the KE, which can give rise to tensions or contradictions (Tennant, 2005). I see these tensions as hopeful, in that they demonstrate that neoliberalism as a discourse is neither as smooth nor as hegemonic as it seems. An aim of this book, and a dimension of my role as a critical scholar in education (Apple, 2006), is to point out *other* ideas about the PhD that we currently hold and articulate, to counter the totalising effects of the neoliberal KE imaginary, and to show its contradictions. Yet it is not just two discourses, an Enlightenment discourse and a neoliberal discourse, that shape our contemporary understandings of the PhD; there are elements, lurking, of an *even older* idea of a scholar that predates the PhD, but which nonetheless contributes to our understanding of it. It is from this idea that we can trace the lingering hint of an affinity with arcane knowledge, as discussed in Chapter 1, and with magic and the esoteric, that recur in contemporary constructions of doctoral researchers.

Ideally, the self that is formed by the end of the PhD is the proper autonomous PhD subject, mixed with the gold standard knowledge worker. Efforts to foster this outcome and to produce the good doctoral subject occur through various practices, coercive and gentle: supervision, institutional reporting, academic development workshops, writing groups and other forms of socialisation, some of which the next chapter will discuss. Interestingly, despite the growth in this area – the attention now paid to doctoral-student-formation – many of these initiatives still rely on the individual taking responsibility for his or her own development as a researcher. Discursively, the individual is hailed (Althusser, 1994/1971) as a particular kind of subject who will undertake technologies of the self (Foucault, 1977).

As we know from accounts of doctoral attrition earlier this century (Golde, 2000, 2005), however, there are other outcomes for the PhD than the independent scholar-academic, or 'enterprising self' (Tennant, 2005). This chapter will introduce the figure of the esoteric student interested in research that is unsupervised and unsanctioned, whose very existence both *haunts* and threatens to destabilise the proper, good doctoral self. The next chapter will return to 'improper' PhD subjects in the context of the supervisor/student relationship. These other PhD scholars consistently reappear in the PhD imaginary, and are particularly visible in popular culture. Although they do not often appear in institutional discourses, at least not overtly, their existence is implied and registered in numerical terms – usually as non-completion statistics. Arguably, these other PhDs are also constructed by institutional discourse by their very repression or *non*-representation, as the articulation of successful graduates depends on an idea of its opposite. This chapter acknowledges the good PhD's other, and considers where resistance to technologies of the (good) self occurs in the figures of bad doctoral researchers, some of whom opt *not* to be good citizens in either traditional academic or contemporary neoliberal terms, but who, sometimes quite deliberately and even contentedly, opt for the irrational or the unprofitable.

Underpinning this chapter is an engagement with ideas about what constitutes the individual subject. As outlined in the Introduction, a fundamental premise of this book is that language and discourse contribute to the formation of subjectivities. Since the mid- to late twentieth century, the notion that identity *is* constructed has engendered a shift away from an idea of a stable self, or Judeo-Christian soul, to one of subjectivity. Various discourses, which could be clustered under the term postmodernist, and which have been influenced by Lacanian psychoanalysis, have contributed to this shift. At the same time, the idea of a *self*, a thinker, reasoned and contemplative, *is* apparent in recent writings about the PhD, perhaps because the Doctor of Philosophy is in some fundamental sense an Enlightenment construct. One element of doctoral subjectivity that increasingly appears in contemporary discourse, despite the old Enlightenment split of mind and body, is the embodied dimension.

The ideal doctoral researcher

At the turn of this century an influential article on doctoral education was published that analysed the idea of the PhD and the autonomous self (Johnson *et al.*, 2000). Traditionally, according to the authors, a successful outcome of a PhD is a graduate who is autonomous in his or her *use of reason* and possesses the attribute of *independence*. The authors describe the development through the course of the doctorate of the traditional figure of the scholar, a figure that persists in informing our ideas about the PhD.

Although I use the term 'traditional', what these authors actually describe is the modern, Enlightenment subject, the ideal of the PhD scholar that dates from the degree's conception in the late eighteenth and early nineteenth centuries. This figure, according to Clark (2006), is the research university personified, the new hero of knowledge, whereas the *traditional* academic was the inhabitant of the early-modern university. Clark is drawing here on what he terms the heuristically simplified idea of the traditional university that was monastic and guild-like, and which he contrasts to the modern research university informed by industrial and bureaucratic practices (Clark, 2006). The traditional academic was a passionate, collegial and somewhat nepotistic academic self, whereas the modern researcher was (is) a more objective, meritocratic professional who has suppressed passion and interest. Drawing on the work of Max Weber, Clark refers to the 'modern schizophrenia' of the new professional, brought about by bureaucratic and capitalist interest, who eschewed the private self and was willing to alienate himself or herself from labour in order to *be* the public expert. The concerns of the market played a critical role in bringing about the new kind of academic: Clark sees the review process and academic publishing as an instrument of the market which helps to establish the reputation of the research academic and his or her charisma. Crucially, according to his argument, this is a different kind of charisma from that which is associated with magic and the esoteric (as discussed in the previous chapter); rather, this charisma arises *out of* rationality. What interests me here is the extent to which the rational scholarly self and its other, which bears some kinship to the Romantic genius, are simultaneously at odds *and* entwined.

To examine the construction of the Enlightenment hero of knowledge in discourse, Clark analyses academic material practices from the period, a methodology enabled by the ascendency of writing and the bureaucratization of the university which produces catalogues, charts, tables, dissertations and so on. Turning now to a *contemporary* product (and instrument) of university bureaucracy, I analyse an institutional text which focuses on the construction of the ideal doctoral researcher. The text is a graduate profile for doctoral graduates from a NZ university, one of many readily accessible on the web. The proliferation of these lists of graduate skills or attributes is testament to their function as practices through which institutions contribute to shaping doctoral subjectivities. At the same time, they are a signifier of the contemporary university entrenched in an audit culture. Lists of attributes also reveal assumptions and understandings of a student at any given time (Bosanquet et al., 2012). As we can see from the profile, in this particular context – NZ in the twenty-first century – the doctorate is not simply understood to produce a researcher in a particular discipline, a scholar; rather, doctoral education has come to be understood as preparing its graduates for a *range* of research careers, inside and outside of the university. While the attributes of reason and independence are articulated, the drive to produce workers with research skills required by the KE has also contributed to an emphasis on *other* attributes suited to the neoliberal era. Consequently, the doctoral researcher, who is responsible for his or her self-development, must cultivate certain characteristics so as to be able to adapt to different contexts. Among the desirable characteristics for doctoral graduates is flexibility, an attribute for our age, lauded in contemporary neoliberal discourse (Shore and Wright, 1999).

The main function of the profile is to describe a set of attributes that are considered, by the institution, to be attainable by the doctoral graduate. The profile is produced in an institutional context: it is written by committee as a companion text to other profiles (at other degree levels) and it draws on institutional texts like the PhD statute and other policy documents relating to the degree. The readers of the doctoral profile are multiple, and include doctoral students, supervisors, employers, the community and other institutions. There are five key attributes that a doctoral candidate will possess according to this profile: specialist knowledge, effective communication, general intellectual skills and capacities, independence, creativity and learning, and ethical and social understanding, each of which is broken down into greater detail. Rather than examine each in turn, I want to focus on how the doctoral researcher is conceptualised overall in this text.

A strong message of the text determines doctoral education at this institution in terms of the educational project that Johnson *et al.* (2000) describe as having its basis in the Enlightenment: that is, forming the ideal doctoral graduate who is the autonomous and independent scholar. Bound up with the Enlightenment project is the idea that a doctoral researcher must attain 'mastery of a body of knowledge', as it is described in the profile. I want to highlight several points about this phrase. The first is the metaphor 'body of knowledge' in this context. Although metaphor is not conventionally a characteristic of informational texts like the profile (McGann, 1991), which is meant to carry a unified message (and has a stated purpose to do so), clearly it is utilised here. The use of the phrase 'mastery of a body of knowledge' not only demonstrates the presence of metaphor, but also shows that the profile, like all written texts (Bakhtin, 1981), is intertextual and draws heavily on other texts: this familiar phrase has not been coined by the committee that wrote this profile; rather, the familiarity of the metaphor 'body of knowledge' is so great that we cease to see it as one.

This particular metaphor has a long discursive history and employs a familiar structure of juxtaposing opposing terms, one privileged above the other. My reading is here influenced by deconstruction, which Jonathan Culler (1997) neatly defines as a critique of the 'hierarchical oppositions' that structure Western thought. Feminist theorist Hélène Cixous (1993: 63–64) has argued that pairs of opposing terms are constructed within the same system of binaries, a persistent 'double braid' ubiquitous in discourse, and which is related to *the* pair man/woman: 'Always the same metaphor: we follow it, it carries us, beneath all its figures, wherever discourse is organised'. A deconstructive reading of paired terms in the graduate profile considers the relationship between ascendant and relegated terms, recognises the presence of silent or implied terms, and considers the relationship between different terms that occupy the same position in the binary:

- independence/dependence
- disciplined/undisciplined
- thinking/feeling
- ethical/immoral
- master/servant or subjugated
- mind/body.

The implicit, associated silent terms facilitate the meaning of the explicit, expressed terms, according to this mode of analysis. We cannot really understand 'master' without a concept of 'servant'. Thus, a deconstructive reading reveals that the idea of the doctoral scholar this profile draws on is the traditional Enlightenment figure described by Johnson *et al.* (2000): male, rational, disciplined, thinking, powerful and independent. *Mastery*, to return to the metaphor, conveys the extent to which this figure of the scholar is in control: as master of that undisciplined and unruly body of knowledge, the doctoral scholar has power over it, as well as understanding of it, and so has risen above the risk of being swamped by knowledge or overwhelmed by uncertainty (Barnacle and Dall'Alba, 2013).

The profile also constructs a doctoral graduate who is independent due to his or her capacity for *self-development*. It identifies 'a strong willingness to seek continuous improvement in research skills', indicating that the doctoral graduate gains the capacity for self-improvement *beyond* the degree as much as the research skills necessary to complete it. The doctoral researcher is, in these terms, able to recognise aspects of himself or herself that are in need of improvement, implying a level of self-awareness (or self-mastery). The profile identifies that the doctoral graduate will possess self-awareness to identify not only the skills he or she needs and requires, but also an 'ability to market these appropriately in the employment market'. So not only does the researcher need a self-reflective capacity, but also knowledge and understanding of the *employment market*. This is the enterprising self that Tennant (2005) describes. Ideally, balancing both these capacities, the doctoral graduate will display (as the profile iterates) 'self discipline and an advanced ability to plan and achieve goals (both personal and professional), including career advancement and identifying appropriate opportunities in the chosen field'.

According to dictionary defition, the terms self-development and self-awareness (along with self-discipline, self-reliant and self-help) have acquired common usage since the nineteenth century. As claimed by Collini (2007), in nineteenth-century Britain the 'independence' acquired a new value and greater force as *progress* came increasingly to define the nation. In the economic and social context of the mid-nineteenth century, an individual character was valued if it was able to avoid dependence and to be self-maintaining. The interest in the formation of character during this era, together with iterations of the (stoic) ideal of self-command (Collini, 2007), are found not only in the popular genres of biography and the *bildungsroman* (novels of self-development) like those by George Eliot and Charles Dickens, but also in the new genre of improvement texts, such as the popular *Self-help* (1859) written by Samuel Smiles.

Self-help, like its prodigious offspring, the self-help manual of the late twentieth century, shares with biography what Booth (2002) describes as a common trope of the genre of self-help manuals – the lists of rules and attributes.

According to Booth, this form of itemisation, utilised in lists of graduate attributes, promises improvement *and* 'good things' to the 'good people' – those who subscribe to the list, and who are able to be self-reliant. These 'good things' include not only happiness, but also business prosperity, which neatly reconciles the individual interests with those of society, ever aiming to build and grow its economy. Like nineteenth-century self-help manuals, and to some extent twentieth-century versions (although these tend to emphasise individual personality and competition over social good (Booth, 2002), the profile harnesses the interests of the doctoral graduate with the interests of the society to which he or she contributes. By tying the personal capacity of the individual to professional achievement, the profile recalls the nineteenth-century ideology of progress of the nation and its economy, as expressed by Smiles (1859): 'National progress is the sum of individual industry, energy, and uprightness'. The repetition of 'advanced' twelve times throughout the profile contributes to the expression of this ideology, although it literally refers to the level of the doctoral degree as advanced beyond undergraduate and masters level. That the doctoral graduate achieves goals that are 'personal and professional', and is able 'to make potentially innovative and important contributions to the communities and societies in which they reside', supports the claim made by Johnson et al. (2000) that the practices of doctoral education seem to resolve a conflict between the imperatives of individual freedom and social integration. This recalls Clark's (2006) account of the modern professional research academic, who must eschew private interests: in this instance, the split is overcome and reconciled, or so it seems.

There are two related ways in which the doctoral graduate profile reconciles the needs of the individual with the social. The first is to do with the contribution of research to economic development and progress. The emphasis on innovation conflates the (old) goal of a doctorate as producing original research, discussed in Chapter 1, with a (new) goal to contribute to the progress and advancement of society through knowledge production. This is increasingly familiar language. As Thomson and Walker (2010: 14) point out:

> New theories of economic growth have conferred on education, on knowledge production and the knowledge society (having replaced the older industrial model) a central role as an essential engine of development.

The profile demonstrates that innovation and commercialisation in research are key factors in the latter's importance to universities, as they are to governments. Just as the language of audit in university discourse has become so pervasive that it is no longer challenged (Shore and Wright, 1999), so has language that posits the purpose of higher education as contributing to the advancement of the economy and the production of economic subjectivities (Saltmarsh, 2011). In his account of *doctoral* education, Peter Bansel (2011) argues that the conceptualisation of the contemporary doctoral scholar is increasingly posited within this narrow economistic frame. This frame, which is discursive, is what Grossman's (2012) researcher-detectives Margaret and Edward struggle to reconcile themselves with: how does their experience of research and discovery, understanding, love and a desire to know *fit* with the language of money, business and commercial interest?

The second reconciliation of the personal with the social in the profile has more to do with ethics than with economics. The world the doctoral graduate enters is 'local and global'. Its local situation, NZ, means the document recognises a 'special responsibility' under the Treaty of Waitangi/Te Tiriti o Waitangi, and globally it is characterised by diversity. The doctoral graduate who participates in the local and global society possesses 'ethical and social understanding', integrity and 'respect for the values of individuals and different cultural groups'. Nussbaum (1997) has described the role of higher education, in particular the humanities, in 'cultivating humanity' to have qualities, ethics, morality that are humanistic in value, echoing the concept of *bildung*, and to an extent that is at work here. Is this ideal compatible with the discourse described above? In their discussion of doctoral education and the larger purposes that it serves *and* furthers, Thomson and Walker (2010) describe the existence of a discursive tension – consistently reiterated in discourse about the doctorate, but also true of the discourse about higher education in general (Collini, 2007) – between the idea that doctoral education promotes public good (enriching for the individual and society) and the rhetoric of businesses and markets, underpinned by the regulatory audit culture. Although, as they argue, the latter discourse in general appears to be overtaking the former, both inform the doctoral profile's account of the 'good' doctoral researcher.

Endgame: the fully developed researcher

If the profile constructs an ideal doctoral graduate student as a responsible economic subject, how is this imaginary carried through in depictions of researchers and early career academics? One construction appears in an advertisement for doctoral study which has a *finished* PhD as its (literal) poster boy; the institution (or its marketing team) utilises the figure of the fully-fledged PhD, the end result of the programme, to highlight its virtues.

If the doctoral profile exhibits tensions between competing discourses, similar tensions are at work in an advertisement for doctoral study produced by another NZ university. It is part of an overall campaign that ran from 2011–2012 and appeared on buses, in magazines, on billboards and in newspapers around the country, with particular targeting in the North Island, for an institution in the South Island. As with the profile, formal considerations of this text, the fact that it has both a graphic and linguistic element which work together to produce meanings aids analysis. How is the researcher conceptualised in this text intended for a more overtly external or public audience, and how does it resemble, or differ from, the doctoral profile?

Straight away, the global is evoked with reference to the plateau of Spain which is 'a long way from the South Island's braided river valleys' (University of Otago, 2011). The background of the researcher, Mariano, who is Spanish, conveys the connectedness of research, of links between NZ and other parts of the world. At the same time, the significance and value of his research as contributing to the local context – 'New Zealand's unique wildlife' – is also emphasised. In the imagery, the researcher's involvement in developing advanced technology with commercial potential are evoked through the tracking devices attached to each hedgehog, and the usefulness of his research – protecting or conserving wildlife from the threat of introduced species – is iterated. Mariano himself could be read as an 'introduced' element, and while I assume there is no such irony present in the text, there is an implicit tension between local and global that the images underscore. The feral animals (cats, as well as hedgehogs) are all introduced to NZ – they are non-native species – so the difficulties or problems (like species trafficking) that arise from movement and interaction on a global scale are evoked. However, these cannot be explicitly acknowledged in this text, which relies on its celebration of the figure of the *global researcher* and the potential of the research to have relevance and applicability beyond the local context. In other words, the intended message of the advertisement is to celebrate the traversing of geographical boundaries, as exemplified by a global researcher, but a contradictory subtext is that there are threats produced by movement across geographical or ecological borders.

The advertisement also celebrates this researcher's interdisciplinarity and his desire to push traditional disciplines into new fields. This form of innovation – shifting 'the boundaries of what we know' – exemplifies definitions of doctoral researchers as seeking new knowledge. The geographical imagery – the use of the well-known metaphor of disciplines as fields – both denotes the area of research and contributes to the impression of boundaries (research or disciplinary but also national or geographical) being crossed by the researcher.

As well as combining fields, the researcher in this advertisement combines the professional with the personal, as described in the doctoral graduate profile. Mariano's 'passion' and 'background in information technology' come together in his research, implying he is a well-rounded self, able to bring *life* and *work* together. The rhetoric of a split between personal and professional, familiar from nineteenth-century discourse, recurs in both the profile and the advertisement. And, like the nineteenth-century *bildungsroman*, the advertisement also conveys a narrative of personal development. This doctoral researcher is on a trajectory, as the journey evoked at the start is both literal (from Spain to the South Island of NZ) and metaphorical: he's come a 'long way'. A key message of the advertisement is that doctoral research at this institution contributes to the formation of a global citizen, who successfully combines personal and professional life and is innovative, passionate, ethical, makes a social contribution and succeeds in a world characterised by new technologies and a global level of interaction. Mariano represents the end goal of the PhD.

As a scientist, Mariano is particularly well suited to contemporary research values. The prioritisation of science, technology, engineering and mathematics (STEM) disciplines in contemporary governmental – and therefore institutional – discourse, with its attendant monetary stake, means that doctoral research in particular fields is often valorised over that in other fields. One of the ways in which potential students are encouraged to be good neoliberal subjects is to make *good choices* about the subject areas they pursue in graduate study. This kind of encouragement is fairly ubiquitous in government policy, and is echoed in media reports on higher education. One example is the 2013 NZ Ministry of Education (MoE) report (Mahony et al., 2013) on what young people earn after tertiary education. The report states that its purpose is to twofold: to help young people make decisions about careers based on finding out about what they will earn, and to provide information for government so it can understand the investment it makes in higher education.

Discussing this report in an article in the NZ media, the Minister for Tertiary Education, Skills and Employment, Steven Joyce, commented on the (good) choices that he hoped young people will make in response to the findings in the report. There are two main issues that he highlights: the first relates to the *field of study* and the second to the *level of study*. The article quotes Mr Joyce as predicting a move away from certain disciplines, including fine arts and performing arts, toward other more 'career-oriented' fields, and foresees that students will also complete higher degree levels. The benefits of this trend would be both personal – as students would have better 'prospects' and also higher earnings (it quotes average income statistics for bachelors', masters' and doctoral degrees) – and it would be good for the economy, in the view of Mr Joyce. Those studying at higher levels are, according to government findings, less likely to be 'on a benefit' or income support. The article ends with Mr Joyce saying that while the idea of 'following your dreams' is still relevant, to an extent, there is a new *realism* reflected in students' ability to make 'good choices' and take into account both their future earnings and their industry competitiveness worldwide (O'Callahan, n.p.). Apparent in the report and the minister's comments to the media is the discourse of individualism that locates responsibility for success – or by implication, failure – in the person of the individual. The report encourages young people, and their parents, who are also named as readers, through the choices they make in higher education to shape themselves as good economic subjectivities – as high earners, not dependent on government support. This final point is underscored by the finding in the report that not only are fewer graduates of higher level degrees 'on a benefit', but also that 'good careers are associated with better health, better well-being and more satisfying lives' (Mahony et al., 2013: 1).

Individualism is so entrenched in current discourse that it is hegemonic, cast as common sense, or something that any sensible person will agree with. Drawing on the work of Foucault (1977), Butler (1997) and Althusser (1971), Youdell (2004) points out that the discourse of individualism simultaneously hails subjectivities *with* common sense and *as* productive, so that we shape ourselves according to these truths. As Bansel (2011), writing specifically about the shaping of doctoral subjectivities, puts it, the perceived needs of the society are discursively reconfigured in terms of individual need. So, according to the advertisement and the MoE report, a good doctoral student is one whose research in a sensible discipline will lead to a satisfying career and earn the graduate a good income, which in turn facilitates his or her good heath, is for the public good, and will contribute to the KE. (Conversely, a 'bad' doctoral research project is not going to serve the economy, nor contribute to high-earning careers for the researcher, which in turn implies he or she will not enjoy good health, well-being and a satisfying life. Take that performing artists!) An important point that Bansel (2011) makes is that the reconfiguration of the individual subjectivity is deeply internalised and cast in psychological terms. Human potential and the increase of capital are neatly aligned, hitching to the personal the political, passion to productivity. Our lives, according to the minister, will be more *satisfying* if we make certain choices.

While the good PhD student might be increasingly couched in this narrow utilitarian frame (Bansel, 2011), there is another, related, idea of the good student that also underpins discursive constructions of the doctoral student. Grant (1997) and Llamas (2006) have described the good student of contemporary higher education as one who is docile, recognises and adheres to the rules, is self-regulating, and is rewarded through mechanisms such as graduation and similar rituals of academia. The *viva voce* for the PhD, which is both examination and rite of passage in one (Kelly, 2009) rewards the successful candidate in these terms.

Rituals like the PhD *viva* are also where we find remnants of the old university that predates the modern research university. The oral exam is the occasion at which the doctoral candidate makes his or her bid to truly enter academia, where the written word, inert matter in the form of the thesis, is brought to life, given spirit and breath, through speech. Old dualities are entrenched and revisited, and, on this occasion the Judeo-Christian privileging of the non-corporeal prevails, in spite of our rationalism. Many countries (though not all, Australia is one exception) keep this academic ritual. The retention of the *viva*, along with other highly ritualised academic traditions and practices like graduation, in which things like academic dress, the procession, and the occupation of the town by the gown (university students) on certain days all *matter*, and suggest that an academic imaginary holds strong. The rituals and practices of academia, including the *viva* itself, have symbolic value and consistently reappear in representations.

For doctoral candidate Zack Addy, a character in popular TV crime series *Bones*, the oral examination marks a significant end *and* beginning in his research career. Zack began working in the lab at the Jeffersonian Institute as a doctoral student amid a team of scientists, including his supervisor (US advisor) Dr Temperance Brennan, nicknamed Bones, the slightly eccentric and wealthy forensic scientist and author, who partners with the FBI to solve murders. (There are several kinds of television shows of this type, including *Numb3rs* and *Perception*.) Zack greatly admires his supervisor and what she has achieved. Zack himself is quirky and something of a misfit – even more so than Dr Brennan. According to one character, he is 'pretty brilliant at making contraptions' (series 3, episode 1). On an interpersonal level Zack lacks in empathy, takes statements too literally, and sometimes finds it difficult to relate to people; these are traits he shares with Dr Brennan. He is rational, very thorough in his research and finds *work* rather than *leisure* fun, recalling Prudencia Hart. FBI agent Booth calls him a 'weirdo' but where he sees weirdness, Dr Brennan sees 'genius'.

In season 2, Zack sits his *viva*. His thesis was on the analysis of bone trauma in forensic anthropology. The episode opens with Zack sitting opposite his panel of examiners, one of whom (Constance Wright) is played by Kathy Reichs (the forensic anthropologist and academic who wrote the novels on which the series is based) and one is his supervisor. Like other representations of the PhD oral (see Morrow, 2009), Zack seems powerless and disadvantaged in comparison to his examiners. He sits alone on one side of the room in a chair with no table, shot from a high camera angle, to make him look small, while the panel of five examiners sit on the other, behind a large wooden table strewn with papers. Zack is rather scruffy. He has longish hair, wears jeans and an open shirt; the panel are formally dressed. As the examination wraps up, one examiner (Kathy Reichs' character) asks Zack how he would expect anyone to take him seriously as a working forensic anthropologist, when he looks the way he does. Zack is taken aback, and mystified. Angela, one of the technicians at the Jeffersonian, later explains: 'If you work here, you won't be Brennan's grad student anymore, you'll be a full-blown forensic anthropologist' (series 3, episode 1). The head of the research centre concurs that an important part of the job is appearance, and encourages Zack to reconsider how he looks, as he currently resembles a 'fill-in at a college radio station'. The point they labour is that Zack is about to make a transition from *student* to *researcher* and to the world of work and career, to a professional researcher role. As Angela's comment also suggests, he will be judged on his own terms, and will not have the security of being under Dr Brennan's wing. Recognising this shift, from student to independent, professional colleague, Zack asks Angela to help with a makeover. When Zack's doctoral results are in, he has passed; the new improved Zack has been physically transformed – he wears a suit and has short hair. Angela introduces him to Dr Brennan and the other scientists as: 'your colleague, Dr Zachery Uriah Addy'.

This scene highlights key elements in the transition and shift in identity from student to 'Dr', and (bearing in mind in the particular context of the lab) from subordinate to equal. Zack also *works on himself* and recasts himself as a professional researcher suited to a career in the prestigious Jeffersonian. Zack's physical transformation marks a shift in the level of self-perception: he now regards himself (with a bit of prompting) as having successfully emerged from his doctorate as an independent and autonomous professional researcher.

The concept of professional research roles is both relatively recent and ubiquitous, and casts research degrees in terms of labour and economic prosperity: for the individual and in terms of a contribution to a society's market and economy. The use of 'professional' in the context of doctoral education has been considered in recent years, in terms of its interchangeability with 'generic', in relation to skills (Barnacle and Dall'Alba, 2011), or its use as a moniker for the named or taught doctorates, as a means of further distinguishing them from the PhD (Tennant, 2005). One way in which we can understand current conceptualisations of the PhD is to compare how it is represented in relation to other (newer) kinds of doctorates. In an article in the *Times Higher Educational Supplement* (*TES*) (Gill, 2009), the inference is that the PhD produces researchers pursuing careers in academia, but the named or professional doctorates are for those who aim to contribute primarily to professional practice. One of the interviewees, Bob Burgess, comments that the professional doctorates fit the 'spirit of the age' even more *now* than they did late last century. An interviewee states that while there is perhaps value in philosophical thought, there is also a point at which research has to return to 'real life' (quoted in Gill, 2009). The title of the article is, tellingly, 'Practical knowledge', and its argument primarily rests on a distinction between knowledge that is produced that is *useful*, by professional doctorates, and that which tends to be not useful, by Doctors of Philosophy.

Perhaps Zack's makeover as a fully-fledged PhD, with a title and appearance appropriate to his professional workplace, speaks to an attempt to overcome concerns like those voiced in the *TES*, about the utility of PhDs in the twenty-first century, an era of 'new realism', according to Mr Joyce. Zack's research at the Jeffersonian contributes to society by enabling justice to be meted out. Despite their quirks and antisocial tendencies, and the fact that much of the research takes place in the highly secure and closed laboratory, the team of researchers in the Jeffersonian are not ivory tower, but contribute to making society safer, to do what FBI agent Booth calls 'serv[ing] a larger purpose' out in the world. Although Booth thinks Zack is 'a strange man', he respects that he works for this purpose, and has this desire (series 3, episode 1). In other words, his weirdness is tolerated, even celebrated, because of what it can achieve when harnessed for good. Although *Bones*, like other similar television series, represents researchers as eccentric, it also reinforces their role in promoting public safety. In this way, it presents a powerful construct by harnessing the trope of researchers as odd obsessives *with* a potential for good useful work.

Mad, bad and dangerous to know: the other PhD

If a 'good' doctoral student is one whose research will lead to a good career and earn the graduate a good income; and if it is for the public good, and will contribute to the KE – who or what is this standard defined against? What or who is the good PhD's 'other'? Here I want to consider the idea that embedded in constructions of good doctoral subjectivities *are* those others, some of whom we encountered in Chapter 1. Against the doctoral candidate who completes the degree, and passes the oral exam, there is the accompanying spectre of those who do not complete, or who fail; there must be, for success to mean anything. Likewise, for the doctoral candidate who manages to turn his or her passion (like Mariano) or eccentricity (like Zack) to good, and make a useful or productive contribution to society and the economy, there are those who do not, who reject the choices espoused by government and opt to 'follow their dreams' and do PhDs in subjects like the performing arts, to take the minister's example (O'Callahan, 2013). Although discursive constructions of *other* PhDs are more likely to appear in texts produced *outside* of institutional or governmental discourse – in Cham's comic, in novels, television and film – institutional discourse also sometimes draws on them for its own ends. This is particularly apparent in two advertisements for doctoral study I now turn to.

As universities are situated within a competitive educational marketplace, like schools, and strive to increase numbers of students as well as compete for so-called quality students, they turn to advertising and marketing themselves.

Advertisements for postgraduate study or doctoral programmes, such as the 2011–2012 campaign from the NZ University, discussed above, or websites like the Australian hotcourses.com, draw on recognisable tropes utilised in popular cultural constructions of the doctorate and research. In an advertisement on the Australian hotcourses.com website, the good, economically viable and productive future employee is utilised alongside its other, to broaden the appeal of doctoral study:

> I'll be the first to admit that I am a nerd. In my undergraduate studies, I was always that overzealous student who wanted to get the course essay questions immediately. I was eager to jump straight into the library to grab all the relevant books and spend hours trawling through one esoteric lead or the other, something to put a unique spin on my research papers...
>
> Whether you're in the scientific, medical, cultural or legal fields, the fundamental drive behind undertaking academic research is an inquisitive spirit and thirst for answers to a particular or set of problems.
>
> For some it's the necessary pathway to take in order to proceed into professional research roles... But for others for whom research is not a pathway to a career, academic research may just be an avenue taken to muse on a particular interest, a quest to find, establish or extend upon a certain way of thinking about a subject matter.
>
> Whatever the reason, the extension of human knowledge through original work is the essence of all research. You never know, what started out as a peculiar personal interest may spiral into a radical and important study.
>
> (Li, 2011)

Although this advertisement uses the same ideas as the NZ university advertisement discussed above, namely that research makes a contribution to public good and is important, and that it benefits a researcher in career terms, at the same time it also mobilises, like *Bones*, the idea that research can be esoteric, pleasurable and simply of peculiar personal interest to the researcher. In addition, the author of this statement, apparently an actual PhD student, regards as fundamental to research an 'inquisitive spirit and thirst for answers', recalling the trope of the detective-researcher discussed in the first chapter.

A close cousin of the researcher-as-detective is the CSI type researcher currently ubiquitous on the small screen – like Zack in *Bones*. A second advertisement from the NZ university's 2011 campaign draws on this contemporary cultural construct. Like the advertisements above (truth is stranger than fiction, after all), this one presents an actual PhD student. This student is studying blood markers for time determination of death. The image shows her wearing protective overalls and crouching next to a vivid and viscous looking pool of blood. She appears to be taking samples as part of an investigation. The image represents the scientist out in the world – not solely satisfying this or her personal 'thirst', but also making the world better, safer, healthier. As with *Bones*, the advertisement emphasises the *usefulness* of research and its impact on society. The gothic overtones in the pale face of student, the bright blood on the ground, and the setting of a dark urban alleyway, are visual tropes that also reference crime series like *Bones*. At the same time, these are clues of a potentially unhealthy researcher (McDermott and Daspit, 2005), provoking an assumption that she perhaps avoids sunlight, or is cooped up in designated research spaces or labs. Does she spend more time, like the researchers in the Jeffersonian, with the dead, than the living? When she is out in the world, is it to hang out in dark grimy alleyways? The less healthy elements of research are *part of* the researcher trope utilised here in this university's advertising campaign.

The ambivalence in the idea of the PhD researcher that the advertisement utilises for effect is played out to an extreme in *Bones*. This occurs on two occasions in season 5. In episode 5, the body of a doctoral student and intern is found in the Jeffersonian. As it turns out, she has been killed by her supervisor. When Dr Brennan expresses disbelief that one of their own has committed murder (he has a doctorate and is therefore meant to be governed by rationality), Booth suggests that she is really unsettled because the murder happened *inside* the research space, the 'House of Reason' (series 3, episode 5). The second occasion is the final episode of the season, when it is revealed that Zack has apprenticed himself to a serial killer, a zealot called the Master, who has a desire to eradicate corruption in society by targeting high-profile members of secret societies. In this situation, Zack's attraction to an argument presented logically, his antisocial tendencies, his experience of subjugating himself in a master/apprentice relationship in being supervised by Brennan, and his desire to work for a greater good, contribute to his susceptibility to the Master's cause. Once again, the shock of finding out that one of their own, an inmate of the 'House of Reason', *and* one who has a doctorate is a criminal, working against them from the inside, is deeply unsettling for the team at the laboratory. Their boundaries – between those who are rational and reasoned, who are 'good' and solve crime, and those who are irrational, 'bad' and commit crime – are displaced. Yet Zack's *unhealthy* research tendencies were always there; in fact, they were utilised in his doctoral research.

As the Australian advertisement tells us, research that is driven by an 'inquisitive spirit' or a 'thirst for answers' can exceed known boundaries, lead in esoteric directions, or to overzealous researchers. This trope of the obsessive researcher is ancient, drawing on the figure of the learned sorcerer (Clark, 2006), and has broad cultural appeal – hence its use by universities for marketing purposes. Yet, within it are potentially destabilising associations. As the previous chapter considered, there is a tension at the heart of many of our ideas about knowledge and the PhD which date back to its inception. Bansel (2011) has argued that although knowledge is now primarily cast in terms of productivity, as intellectual capital, it is also understood through a long discursive history to be both dangerous and unsettling. According to Lee and Williams (2005: 6), the PhD is *predicated on* this contradiction: the 'simultaneous production and disavowal of the irrational'. What *Bones* highlights is what Erica McWilliam (2009) refers to as a tension between the 'maverick' behaviour regularly attributed to intellectuals, which is seen as necessary to producing new knowledge, and their more utilitarian function and role within society. Our ideas about the PhD at *this* time are underpinned by this ambivalence.

Doctoral becoming? Imagining alternatives

What happens when these contradictions in ideas about PhD knowledge and researcher-identity are celebrated, rather than suppressed or overcome? To conclude the chapter, I turn to other kinds of recently imagined academic identities, some edgy ideas of the individual subject of knowledge. These imaginings – in some cases *hoped for* subject positions – pose complex understandings of the person-subject that might emerge from or with a PhD. These imaginings resist conforming to not only the narrow utilitarian, economistic idea of the good subject, discussed above, and its rather scary 'other', but also the rational-autonomous subject of the Enlightenment PhD. At least, there is a *degree* of resistance – there is also engagement: both/and. What follows is a series of imaginings presented as provocations: brief articulations of doctoral graduate or early career academic identities that are not neatly defined, and which share some commonalities.[1]

The subject inside/outside neoliberal discourse

One alternative to the idea of the good economistic PhD self is espoused by Peter Bansel (2011), who imagines the possibility of an academic identity that is, by the end of the PhD, positioned both inside and outside the utilitarian frame. This academic identity is purposely ambivalent, or constructed within a rationality of logic *not* predicated on the binary of 'danger and risk'. What this kind of positioning involves, according to Bansel, is an identification of (sometimes resisting, sometimes working with) the processes through which academic identities are overtly formed – in particular, the deliberate practices that universities currently undertake in order to shape 'good' academic subjectivities. For doctoral candidates, these include PhD milestones and the fostering of certain attributes or skills, such as are outlined in the graduate profile the chapter began with.

The doctoral researchers situated within and outside the frame can develop what Davies (2005) refers to as a *doubled gaze* that will enable them to construct stable identities, to survive and thrive as academics or researchers, yet also to counter and critique the worst effects of neoliberalism. In a similar vein, Saltmarsh (2011) has argued for a process of 'undisciplining' the subject of higher education by allowing the complexities and the contradictions in academia to show, allowing for a less *tidy* conception of the academic self to emerge. I considered these issues when, in my former role, I was involved in the design and delivery of a programme for PhD students intending to pursue an academic career (Kelly and Brailsford, 2012). In some ways, this programme aimed to foster the very kind of good academic subjectivity that Minister Joyce would approve of, in that it was directed at career-oriented doctoral students. Yet in other ways, the programme enacted the process that Saltmarsh describes, in that it did reveal some of the complexities and contradictions of academic life and work.

The fragmented academic: in 'bits and pieces'

One impression of academic work, supported by recent higher education research literature, can be that it consists of different roles difficult to reconcile. Although the sense of what Simmons (2011) calls a fractured academic role-identity may be the curse of the new or soon-to-be academic, which resolves over time into a more integrated role, an argument can be made for the fragmentation of academic work being *a sign of the times*. According to Shore (2010), universities currently operate within a frame of contradictory aims and competing discourses: this 'schizophrenic university' is characterised by fragmentation, which has a significant impact on academic subjectivities, pulled in different directions. Stories of trying to reconcile contradictory demands are not uncommon amongst twenty-first-century academics, although, as Clark (2006) shows, 'schizophrenia' is not a condition unique to the contemporary university. Ylijoki's (2008) Dr X describes academic work as having become notably fragmented in recent years, with 'unnecessary' tasks like writing grant applications, filling in forms, responding to enquiries and attending administrative meetings detracting from his 'necessary' work.

Doctoral candidates who were involved in the careers programme outlined above (see Kelly and Brailsford, 2012), picked up on these ideas of the fragmented or 'bitsy' academic from hearing academics talk about their work – yet some reframed the concept in productive terms. One (male, Education PhD) considered the possibility of different elements of 'a teacher, scholar, researcher person' melding into an imagined self who is constantly evolving and learning, rather than a static or finished self. This figure has agency, and is able to produce himself or herself, and 'become someone' – a less pessimistic or passive scenario than is sometimes found in research literature. Another (female, Health/Medicine) conveyed an idea of bringing together different roles within academic work:

> ... my main moment of insight was understanding how all the bits and pieces fitted together ... fitting them altogether to build a picture of what a full academic would be like, I guess. For someone would be talking about ... academic citizenship and someone would come along and talk about teaching, someone would talk about research skills and stuff, so they're all like parts of the body, like different parts. And then at the end I guess the a-ha moment was really fitting them together into the whole *picture*, to build the person, you know the academic person, and learning how to interlink those things together and finding the time to do that ... [Y]ou don't have to keep them all separate, they could all be really interlinked.

On the one hand, the image of different parts of the body suggest at fragmentation, yet on the other, the metaphor indicates that the parts *do fit* and the different roles combine into a complex yet whole 'academic'.

The academic inside/outside the university

What of the academic who exists on the border of the university, or is both an academic, and something else? Although this positioning has potential to fracture a unified academic identity, it can also be seen as a more complex idea of identity that recognises it can be multiply placed in different sites at the same time (Clegg, 2008). One doctoral candidate (female, Health/Medicine) described noticing separations, or differentiation (Clegg, 2008), between clinical and research work, and between the hospital and university. While she sometimes experienced the differentiations as challenging and hard to reconcile, she also developed an enhanced desire to combine them, and talked about her aspiration for future work following the PhD:

> ... I know there aren't really that many hospital [staff] who are publishing full research or integrating it very closely. Because at [my] School ... researchers they tend to be quite separate, they are true academics. ... So I guess I want to be able to ... bring that into mentoring others to do their own research to get them to publish papers and be a more

research active Department. . . . That's what I hope to achieve . . . rather than keeping it *separate* you know just purely University or purely hospital – being able to bridge that gap a bit better . . . I think it really opened my eyes to the way academic life works, and also the limitations as well and the challenges . . . I learnt I don't think I can be a pure academic. But I wouldn't say it made me *not* want to be one, if that makes sense, I just think it needs to be a modified form. A mutated form of academia.

This imagined possibility expresses hope, for this doctoral candidate, of a new way of being in academia that combines or reconciles *different* elements and enables a dual positioning. In the UK, the *Arts and Humanities Research Council's* Collaborative Doctoral Partnership scheme is facilitating research positioning similar to that which is imagined here. In this scheme, doctoral candidates are dually located in, and supervised by, a university and non-higher education institution like a museum or gallery. While the website couches this opportunity in fairly dry terms – as opportunities for training and skills development – the actual projects offer new and exciting ways of imagining and doing arts and humanities research.

The academic outside the university

While some doctoral candidates imagine being multiply sited inside/outside academia, one (male, Education) considered an even more radical positioning: 'Can you be an academic without being in the university? I think that's also open for debate. Because there are people who are scholars who aren't part of the University'. Of course there are scholars, like Galileo, who have (famously) undertaken research outside of the university institution – often, as in Galileo's case, because of a desire to question orthodoxies (Segre, 2015). While *in* the institution, Segre (2015) writes, Galileo laid claim to the title of 'philosopher' because it granted him (unlike 'mathematician') both a higher status and the right to deal with essences. Does the example of Galileo offer an idea of a Doctor of Philosophy at large?

The border-crosser and the rhizomatic researcher

One way of thinking about being multiply placed as a doctoral researcher is less to do with the institution as a site and more to do with being *institutionalised*, or disciplined into the disciplines. One participant in my study, Curtis, (male, Fine Arts/Education) shared his idea and image of the jester or maverick: a researcher who is a border-crosser (Giroux, 1992) and resists both disciplinary boundaries *and* the structuring of thought that belonging to a discipline requires (Foucault, 1994/1970). Enacting a transversal of one specific border, this doctoral candidate works in both word and image: his jester appears in multiple drawings, enacting the candidate's rogue methodology. Similarly, a recent publication that reflects on *and* undermines academia's privileging of the written word in research is *Unflattening* (Sousanis, 2015), the first doctoral dissertation to be written and drawn in comic book form. *Unflattening* opens with an image of higher education as a factory, churning out beings who are largely the same, who all think and act the proper way. According to Sousanis (2015), this is the process of *flattening* – standardising individuals, such as through imposing steps or milestones, curtailing possibilities of thought. To counter, *Unflattening* depicts a rhizomatic way of being, an expansive form of knowing conveyed in the pages of the work. Both these doctoral researcher-artists enact a way of doing research in which image and word are complexly woven – and in which the idea of the doctoral researcher is constructed in line as well as language.

An old idea of higher education as transformative also runs through Sousanis' comic. Not the idea of transformation as self-development (the 'work on yourself until you are a fit subject for the global knowledge economy' discourse described above), but the (admittedly related) idea that higher education has potential to liberate the individual. To liberate from restrictive social mores and norms, as Sousanis (2015) explores, but also to liberate *through* thought, the capacity to reason, and encounters with knowledge – the Enlightenment's legacy.

Knowledge as a way of being and becoming

If knowledge is not simply a thesis or a commodity, possessed by individuals or offered to the university, but is instead (as considered at the end of the previous chapter) something enacted and lived by the doctoral subject, it is then understood as a way of being. An ontological approach to the PhD, such as Barnacle and Dall'Alba (2013) explore (as discussed in Chapter 1), presents an idea of the PhD self (individual) that includes a commitment to risk and unsettling, rather than mastery in the sense of control. In an earlier article, Robyn Barnacle (2005) explores the idea of the Doctor of Philosophy as a lover of wisdom. Drawing on Plato, she considers the figure of Eros, the concept of desire (here, a desire for knowledge and wisdom), and the idea that philosophy is 'perpetual striving'; the implication, Barnacle points out, is that the attainment of knowledge is always partial, unfinished. Picking up on this idea of doctoral identity as *becoming*, rather than *being*, Lenz Taguchi (2013) imagines herself as 'molecular girl', as outlined by Deleuze and Guattari (1987, as cited in Taguchi, 2013). Through this metaphor, Lenz Taguchi offers an understanding of a researcher-subjectivity that is different from the single, stable category 'man' of Western philosophical discourse, in that it is in perpetual movement, unfinished.

The postmodern PhD as vampire

Is the figure of the vampire, discussed in Chapter 1, actually the metaphor *par excellence* for the PhD graduate? McDermott and Daspit (2005) suggest ways in which it could be, drawing on their analysis of the 1995 film *The Addiction*, in which doctoral candidate Kathleen becomes a vampire (and, incidentally, eats her *viva* committee after her successful defence). Starting with a reminder that the seeking of knowledge is both addictive and a form of 'the hunt', according to Michel Serres, the authors tease out further points of connection, of which I highlight several. First, they point to ways in which, through a series of arcane rituals, the identity of the individual is transformed and a 'doctor' emerges. At the same time, this identity, in the contemporary postmodern episteme, can no longer be conceptualised as stable and singular: like the vampire (dead/undead, human/other) it is more than one thing at once, an identity that exceeds the Western either/or construct. In addition, the doctoral candidate, through surrendering himself or herself to the hunt, has undergone an annihilation of self. This erosion of the idea of a stable identity – along with a stable notion of truth and so on – is a form of deconstruction (the vampire is inherently a 'deconstructive figure', according to Hollinger (1997, cited in McDermott and Daspit, 2005) that overturns Enlightenment-era certainties. So the doctoral-student-as-vampire represents the postmodern struggle with the modern: the academics of today must live with the erosion of epistemic and metaphysical certainties.

If this seems a bit grim, the authors offer another idea of a doctoral graduate through their reading of the end of the film: Kathleen has graduated to become a *post-vampire* PhD, who is reconciled to being unfixed and who celebrates her capacity to reshape herself. While the aim of these authors is to celebrate the possibilities that postmodernism allows for rethinking identity categories, including academic identities, this idea of an unfixed and mobile PhD subjectivity bears some resemblance to the *ideal of the flexible worker* valorised for the global KE. Much has been said about the uses of 'flexibility' in neoliberal discourse (Ylijoki, 2008; Lea and Stierer, 2011) and it is a term that we hear often – mostly in relation to a perceived need to be able to diversify oneself, or foster adaptability in career terms. While I have reservations about this term, the kind of subject implied, there are advantages for emerging academics in being able to adapt to different situations. Ideally, as Davies (2005) outlines, students could be *both* adaptable *and* able to produce stable narratives of identity.

The slow academic

While some recent imaginings of doctoral graduate subjectivity fit quite well with the ideal of a neoliberal doctoral-graduate-subject – and celebrate mobility and flexibility – not all do. One doctoral candidate who participated in the academic careers programme (female, Fine Art/Design) considered the unfashionable idea of the university as a place for non-conformists, and imagined a future self as an academic who would opt *not* to strive for excellence, or be competitive, but to simply to live and work and be:

> As I get older and maybe I've started to realise that maybe the university isn't quite the place for nonconformists that it used to be. Like maybe ... you have to be a bit kinda sharper and better dressed and a bit more ambitious and things. I'm not – I don't know if it sounds a bit contradictory for someone who's trying to be an academic to say they're not very ambitious ... I just want to do some research that contributes and teach some people and have good colleagues and have kind of a pleasant life on an acceptable salary.

Studies involving new academics have similarly found resistance to the idea of competitive striving that seems to permeate contemporary academia within an audit culture. Archer (2008) found that some young academics – although resistant to the idea of a golden age of academia, as both untrue and unobtainable – nonetheless also longed for a slower pace and for more *time* to think and do research.

The ethical scholar, contributing to society

The hoped-for figure of the slow academic imagined by a doctoral candidate undertakes activities traditionally valued in the university – teaching, research, making a contribution to society. The last of these, the idea that research could *contribute*, was picked up by another doctoral candidate (male, Education) in the careers programme, who expressed the concern that academics, whom he believed to have a 'moral responsibility' to contribute to their societies and communities, instead seemed to describe their service activities solely in terms of 'bolstering my CV'. As Petersen (2011) points out, the 'what's in it for me' narrative makes sense in a neoliberal context, which tends to emphasise individualism and competition over community (Davies, 2005; Shore, 2010). Nonetheless, despite a myriad of pressures, doctoral candidates *do* resist this narrative. A participant in my study J. T. (PhD student, Education), who is Canadian, wrote that she went into the PhD because the ideal of doing 'service to society' seemed possible:

... through my Master's program, and now the PhD, I learned that there are *other* ways to do research and be an academic and yet still be involved with people in an ethical and humane and meaningful way that attempts to create change ... Academia became more hopeful for me ...

J. T. wrote that she came to see how the PhD might align with her 'values and politics' to contribute to society and effect change. At the same time (and recalling the participants in the careers programme, above), the PhD also seemed to offer the chance to draw on different aspects of herself: 'to combine the more introverted parts of my self (who likes to read, ponder, do analysis and write), the more socially extroverted parts of my self (who likes to organise or facilitate creative group activities) *and* my values'. J. T. conveys optimism, possibility and hope (Clegg, 2008; Archer, 2008) by situating the researcher-self in a community and doing work for society. Yet she also acknowledges dimensions of the researcher-self that are more traditionally associated with the PhD. In J. T.'s imaginary, these elements are not contradictory, or ambivalent, but are productively combined – benefiting the self and the community.

The self in discourse

This chapter has considered means by which discourse – from popular culture and the media to institutional discourse – has a pedagogical potential in shaping particular kinds of educational subjectivities. (Indeed, this book is based on the premise that it is in the wider discursive context which individual doctoral subjectivities are shaped.) Yet there are other ways in which discourse contributes to the shaping of doctoral researchers' sense of self *as an academic* that I have not yet examined here. The first was touched on in Chapter 1, and is to do with writing. According to Eik-Nes (2008), research writing contributes to an individual researcher's disciplinary becoming. Drawing on Goffman's ideas of the presentation of self (1967, 1971), Eik-Nes argues that through experimental 'back-stage' writing, a doctoral student tries out different discursive identity-roles, so that a proper and scholarly 'front-stage' self can be presented in writing that might be for a supervisor's eyes or for publication. Through this mix of back-stage and front-stage writing, a researcher becomes socialised into the academic discipline.

The second, related, means through which a researcher is socialised into a researcher identity through language involves *talk*. According to Mewburn (2011), doctoral students engage in 'troubles talk' as one means of assembling an academic identity. Like the backstage writing that Eik-Nes (2008) describes, troubles talk is not a frontstage activity: although pervasive, it usually happens behind-the-scenes – over the tea tables at a conference, rather than behind the podium. It is also, as Mewburn demonstrates, carried out through online forums, informal doctoral communities that have multiplied this century, and which enable and foster 'troubles talk'. Engaging in this kind of talk, she argues, enables a doctoral researcher to learn about, and *manage*, his or her place in the academic world, similar to the backstage experimentation with a writerly identity that Eik-Nes describes.

The doctoral subject in situ

Although it is not her focus, Mewburn (2011) refers to the ways in which PhD student identity is also formed through its interaction with *things*. The materials of doctoral study (she lists books, identity cards, libraries and computers) foster the development of academic practices and contribute to an individual's sense of how to *be* in academia, just as talk with others does, signalling the material 'turn'. Hopwood and Paulson (2010) have called for further research on the body in doctoral education, arguing that current research tends to construct a PhD student who is disembodied and reduces research to a merely cerebral activity pursued by the mind. Although there is more to be done, a growing strand of research brings the material and the discursive together – as Mewburn (2011) begins to do, in arguing that identity formation occurs through discursive *and* material interactions. Cumming (2007, 2009a, 2009b) and Green (2009) highlight the ways that practices (material and social) are the means by which doctoral candidates develop an identity: Green (2009) gives the example of the doctoral seminar. This kind of socialisation is what I now turn to in the following chapter.

Endnote

1 The data sources for this section are the interviews with doctoral candidates and graduates gathered between 2013 and 14, recent accounts of doctoral identity in research literature, and interview data from another study in 2011. The 2011 data comes from a series of interviews conducted to review a programme for doctoral candidates intending to pursue academic careers. As it was new and enabled by a grant from our university's strategic development funding, my colleague and I conducted interviews from PhD participants in the programme, in order to reflect on its pros and cons. The findings relevant to this review and assessment are discussed elsewhere (Kelly and Brailsford, 2012). What we also found (as something of an unintended consequence) was that some of the candidates, through their experience of the programme, combined with doing a PhD, reflected on ideas of academic identity, 'academic life' and 'the academic person', which I draw on here.

CHAPTER 3

The idea of PhD pedagogy

'Well,' he said, turning to his coffeepot and waving me to a chair. 'How's the opus coming along?' I filled him in on several weeks' work, and we had a short argument about trade between Utrecht and Amsterdam in the early seventeenth century. He served up his fine coffee in porcelain cups and we both stretched back, he behind the big desk. The room was permeated with the pleasant gloom that still came in at that hour, later each evening now that spring was deepening.

(Kostova, 2005: 16)

The whole... supervisor... student... pedagogy operates as a sado-masochistic discourse...

(Dawson, 2010: 151)

How is PhD pedagogy conceptualised in contemporary discourse? Doctoral pedagogy is usually figured as supervision, often, in particular in literature and popular culture, in the traditional dyadic form. Like other kinds of teachers (Gregory, 2007) PhD supervisors seem to hold a fascination, particularly for writers of novels and television dramas. In research literature, the attention garnered by supervision stems from another goal, a sense of needing to be more reflexive about it as a form teaching, usually by showing supervision at work through transcripts of supervisory meetings (Grant, 2008) or through student and supervisor accounts of their experience of supervision. This examination of what is (or was) essentially a private form of teaching has operated in tandem with an increased scrutiny on supervision by institutions, as articulated in institutional policies, and a fostering of self-induced scrutiny through manuals on supervision (Wisker, 2012). Both of these trends are suggestive of a perception at the end of the twentieth century, aided by studies showing high attrition rates and lengthy times to submission (Golde, 2000, 2005), that supervision *was often not going well*.

Accounts of supervision inside the academy have turned our gaze towards a pedagogical practice which was traditionally out of sight, and offer it up for scrutiny, examination and judgement. Depictions outside the academy reveal a fascination with supervision, and a desire to reveal what takes place behind the academy's closed doors.

In popular and cultural discourse, the pedagogical practice of supervision is usually represented as fairly traditional, private and dyadic, conveying and reinforcing what Manathunga and colleagues (2013) term the normalised cultural narratives of supervision. This chapter begins by examining this historically derived idea of supervision as a dyad (Lee and Green 2009), a private practice, between two people engaged in an exchange of ideas, tucked away in rooms. I consider how and why the ancient and traditional model of pedagogy via dialogue (Grant, 2008), epitomised in the Oxbridge tutorial, and which is in reality no longer the only or even primary form of doctoral education, nonetheless dominates in the cultural imagination. I analyse a range of supervisory tropes from the available discursive constructions and offer a partial taxonomy of supervisor stereotypes. I then extend this taxonomy further, in the following section, to analyse several (of the many) representations of supervisory relationships in which issues of gender and power are brought to the fore.

To set against the dyadic model I then explore ideas of doctoral pedagogy in groups, usually (though not exclusively) a PhD imaginary located in the domain of the sciences. As I consider, representations of lab groups and research groups epitomise the idea that doctoral pedagogy involves learning how to *be* in academia via socialisation and enculturation into the discipline. As discussed in the previous chapter, doctoral education can be understood as a form of preparation for academia, or of the formation of scholars in a disciplinary field. Although this analysis focuses on discourse it draws on practice theory to help interpret the ways in which doctoral pedagogy is *represented* as a social practice. Schatzki's (2002) account of social orders helps us reflect on how types and roles that we find in stories of doctoral pedagogy offer ideas about how pedagogical relations in the university, specifically the texture of relationships in doctoral education, work. As I argue, the other way in which PhD pedagogy can be understood as fundamentally social comes from Green (2005), who writes that pedagogy is far more than just teaching and is inextricably tied to 'social dynamics of learning'. He offers the term 'ecosocial' to situate PhD pedagogy, to highlight the broader environment within which postgraduate study is undertaken. In this chapter I look at the pedagogy of the PhD in terms of its figuring as situated in a social context or milieu.

Further, I draw on another understanding of ecosocial from Green (2005): the idea that PhD pedagogy happens in a *field of identification*. This is another sense in which the PhD can be understood environmentally, for instance through the available images of pedagogy, in particular supervision, that shape our expectations (Green, 2005). Manathunga and co-authors (2013) describe not only the physical but also *metaphorical* locations in which supervision occurs, and which constrain us, as 'supervisor' and 'student' – which says something of this broader environment that I am calling the PhD imaginary. Metaphorical locations for and of supervision are discursive and contribute to an ideological context within which doctoral pedagogy takes place. As outlined in the previous chapters, the current field of identifications for doctoral pedagogy is broad and diversely located.

The dyadic inheritance: private pedagogy

In his memoir *Sandstone Gothic*, Andrew Reimer (1998) recalls his arrival in the UK as a doctoral scholar in the mid-twentieth century. Significant in this memory is an encounter with his potential supervisor. Reimer's account draws on and reinforces the pedagogy of 'magisterial disdain' and 'pedagogy of indifference', which seem to characterise many imagined or remembered accounts of PhD supervision. In Reimer, this perceived attitude is reinforced by the austereness and desirability of the supervisor's wood-panelled and well-appointed rooms, which are in stark contrast to the author's own humble student dwelling. The trope of the supervisor enclosed in Oxbridge-like rooms is familiar to the point of being clichéd. And yet, new versions of this trope were particularly prolific at the start of this century, and continue to be produced. What is the genealogy of this figure of the enclosed supervisor in a wood-panelled study, inaccessible to all but a privileged few? What can we *see* of pedagogical practices in these imagined accounts?

The figure of the supervisor in the cultural imagination of the PhD is a recognisable type: stern, often paternal, always in authority. In the following taxonomy of fictional supervisor stereotypes within that frame, one has elements of a parental figure, one is positioned in the role of master in a master-servant dynamic (Grant, 2008), and the third is defined by a cultural and epistemological divide between a fairly traditional critical English supervisor and a theoretically oriented (and poststructuralist to boot) American student. Although what is presented here can be seen to form an incomplete taxonomy of supervisory types, recalling Green's (2005) restricted series within a symbolic hierarchy, the figures of the supervisors should also be recognised for the function they perform in each of the three texts as a foil to the graduate research student. While they are different, all three of these texts produce and sustain a binary of 'student' and 'supervisor', paired terms that are able to be mapped onto other oppositional pairings (self/other) mobilised by the generic conventions that each text draws on, and in some cases, subverts.

Here, I focus on three texts from popular culture that represent supervision with a degree of satire: recent novels by A. S. Byatt and A. N. Wilson and an online comic strip by Jorge Cham. Two of the texts, the novels by Wilson and Byatt, come out of a tradition of post-war British university fiction, and both represent graduate students of English literature. By contrast, Jorge Cham's narrative of postgraduate life is an online comic, first started in 1997 and still in production, based on Cham's own experience of the North American graduate school system. Unlike Byatt and Wilson, Cham is not a graduate of an arts or humanities discipline, and nor is his central character. What these three texts share is that they are recent fictions, published this century, which portray the 'private' practice of supervision and which draw on, and contribute to, supervisory tropes.

The first type in this brief taxonomy is the supervisor in *loco parentis*. A. S. Byatt's *The Biographer's Tale* (2000) is like all of Byatt's novels, in that its setting includes a university environment. In *Possession: A Romance* (1990), for instance, Byatt combines the genres of romance and mystery with university fiction. The central character in *Possession*, Roland Michell, is an unlikely hero and literary sleuth, who considers himself excluded from the discipline of literary studies by his old-fashioned approach to literature, and who still suffers from his 'discouraging experience' of being supervised for his doctoral research by the gruff Professor Blackadder (Byatt, 1990). Unlike the satisfyingly conclusive *Possession*, *The Biographer's Tale* is a riddling narrative by another research sleuth of sorts, a biographer, whose pursuit of his elusive subject, another biographer, forms the inconclusive narrative. While this novel is primarily a satire of biography, and reflects Byatt's mistrust of that genre's ability to capture the truth of its subjects, it nonetheless also takes opportunities to critique and satirise research practices and doctoral pedagogy in a university context.

The Biographer's Tale begins with Phineas Nanson experiencing an epiphany and renouncing his research project in the area of literary theory. Phineas decides he wants a life of *things* not words, and craves release from 'theoretical pedagogy'. As something of an aside, he mentions that his mother has recently died, causing him to miss the seminar on *Frankenstein*; two pages later he comments, again in passing, on his father's disappearance (Byatt, 2000). Although Phineas makes no connection between these events and his decision, the reader can, if primed to look for gaps and evasions in texts. Phineas' deliberately offhand remarks on the loss of his parents provide an early clue to the real subject of this tale: despite his attempts to efface himself from the narrative, Phineas, the I, creeps back in, revealing that the biographer's tale is in fact an autobiography, a novel of Phineas' own self-development (like the *bildungsroman* referred to in the previous chapter). At the same time, this brief aside also points the reader to Phineas' untrustworthiness as a narrator and teller of (truthful) tales. Similarly, what are the implications for *research* if Phineas is not that ideal researcher: the objective and omnipresent I?

After the seminar, Phineas announces his intention to the Head of Department, Professor Goode, and over a whiskey the two of them consider Phineas's options, prompting him to start a new research project – a biography of a biographer, facts being the closest thing that a literary scholar can come to *things*. Having divested himself of one supervisor and one research topic within the frame of a particular paradigm, Phineas reconstitutes himself and turns to quite another supervisor and topic, and to quite a different theoretical framework, one that seems more safe and solid. Phineas's two potential supervisors are each representative of what Gonzalez considers inseparable contraries within English studies (2008): their uneasy and strained alliance in the seminar and Phineas's defection from one to the other are indicators of the oft-depicted crisis or schism in literary studies that appears in so many campus novels (Birrer, 2007), including others by Byatt. Certainly, Goode's loathing for theory is exactly what appeals to Phineas at this point, although this neat division, between theory and criticism, is not a binary that the novel will sustain. Phineas's swift and radical shift in topic also serves as a warning sign for supervisors, in Manathunga's terms (2005), flagging the potential for difficulties ahead.

The next time Phineas meets with his new supervisor is their first pre-arranged meeting since the heady whiskey-infused and rather celebratory meeting that followed Phineas's change in heart and change of topic. Although less effusive than at their first meeting, the supervisor and student, over a sherry this time, come to an arrangement. Goode suggests that Phineas should do a bit of 'detective work', which Phineas immediately agrees to do, despite having previously avoided this kind of scholarly sleuthing. As Head of Department, Goode is an authoritative figure, and Phineas, who has lost both parents, seems to *want* direction and authority at this point. Goode makes the decisions for both of them – from what they will drink, to the research project that Phineas will pursue. At this point in the novel, Byatt draws on a traditional notion of the supervisor-student relationship, one that Grant (2005) has termed the classic master-disciple relation, whereby the student depends on the authority and experience of his or her supervisor. In physical terms, Goode is a large man, whereas Phineas himself is small; Phineas almost has to run to keep up with Goode in the corridors. Phineas is uncertain and fond of vacillating – he is without a clear purpose. Adrift, he welcomes the firm and guiding force that Goode initially offers.

Despite the surety of this beginning, and despite Goode's firm hand, Phineas' project never quite comes together, and he is unable to impose an order on the *things* that he discovers. Phineas' research leads him in more directions than he can possibly pursue, he starts 'too many hares' and finally reaches a point where he has no idea what to do next. At the same time, his income is diminishing, along with his contact with other human beings, and so he goes to see his supervisor. This time, there are no drinks and Goode seems to Phineas to be rather detached, as if his expectations of Phineas' project are waning. At the same time, the reader can see that the supervisor *is* concerned: he asks Phineas what he does in his spare time and tells him he does not look very well, that he should take a break. Phineas finds this intrusive and thinks that Goode has no right to enquire about his personal life. Phineas is uncomfortable with a shift in the relationship from the traditional master-disciple mode to one that is more personal, resembling what Grant (2005) calls the psychological mode in which the supervisor offers support to the student. And yet, when asked about how his research is progressing, Phineas is unresponsive – he cannot think of what to say, or how to convey in any robust and believable way the importance of his rather 'mad' discoveries and their tenuous connections (Byatt, 2000).

From this point, Goode is largely absent from the narrative. Occasionally, Phineas mentions his intention to meet with him, but the meeting is always contingent on finishing something, which never quite happens. Eventually, near the close of the novel, Phineas decides to meet with his supervisor. Neither student nor supervisor finds this a satisfactory conversation. Phineas feels he has done a great deal of work, but worries that he has little to show for it. Goode does not make the connections between the three different lives that Phineas has examined, nor can he understand their significance for the project, partly because Phineas has been unable to convey it. Phineas undervalues the work he *has* done, because he has not been able to produce something to show the supervisor: something finished, concrete, a *thing*.

Phineas does not finish the dissertation. His tendency to pursue more than one thing at once is not overcome and his project maintains no clear direction, or coherence. The novel celebrates rather than laments this, however, and closes with Phineas happily living out two seemingly contradictory lives both at once, still writing, but having bid a farewell to his thesis project and to his supervisor. The gradual disappearance of the safe and solid Ormerod Goode from Phineas' narrative reflects the text's engagement with the genre of biography and autobiography, and indicates that Phineas has reached maturity, and has no need for an authoritative figure like his supervisor. In a final twist, however, Byatt's novel closes not with Phineas' achievement of independence as a researcher or articulation of a single, stable identity, but with his refutation of those achievements as meaningful.

The second type in this brief taxonomy is the supervisor-as-master who appears in *Piled Higher and Deeper* (*PhD Comics*) by Jorge Cham (1997-).

As an online comic, the form and structure of *PhD Comics* is of course quite different to a novel, and comics, in general terms, operate with different conventions and different practices of publication to the literary novel today. In the case of this comic, the individual strips each have a title and a narrative, and each takes its own form: four frames, three frames, sometimes one. The strips appear separately, but are part of a larger comic that has no clear narrative direction: *PhD Comics* is endless and meandering, like the projects of its protagonists. There are several central characters, all of whom are pursuing graduate study in different fields. One of them is the everyman or nameless hero of the strip, and it is with this character's entry into a graduate science programme that the comic began in 1997.

An early strip, 'Research Independent Study' (Cham, 17 November 1997), introduces the topic of supervision. The keen candidate approaches the desk of the unseen supervisor, here termed advisor, with the hope of discussing a research project with him, only to be knocked back by a rather brusque response from a disembodied voice. In the second strip from this era ('Research Independent Study', Cham, 19 November 1997), the student is now working on his independent project with Dr Smith: he is washing the lab's windows. The advisor has allowed entry, but the student is given only the most menial of tasks. In one of the studies on the doctorate in the USA that has come out of the Carnegie initiative, the student research participants construct similar narratives to Cham's comic: the authors describe how students are sometimes treated as 'cheap labour' for an advisor's current project or 'exploited' as lab technicians or low-paid tutors and instructors (Walker *et al.*, 2008). Both of these strips, like many others that are published in the comic, depict a traditional idea of an advisor: he is male, he is usually found behind a desk; he issues instructions that he expects the student to carry out; he is not interested in other aspects of the student's life; he is unsympathetic and he is without personality. All this indicates that he exists in the realm of the symbolic: he is an unreal, fantasy figure that represents authority whom Green (2005) might term the Subject of Knowledge. His name is Dr Smith.

Dr Smith is conventionally unapproachable. At a Christmas party in 'Schmoozing with your Professor' (Cham, 10 December 2007), the hero and Dr Smith find themselves having to interact socially: the student is awkward, and guilty at being away from the lab; Dr Smith is virtually silent, and disapproving. Like Phineas in Byatt's novel, Cham's hero experiences unsatisfactory meetings with Dr Smith. The supervisor seems not fully aware of *who* the student is, or in *what* project he is involved. In 'What have I been doing?' (Cham, 10 April 1999), the unnamed hero impresses Dr Smith with his zeal in wanting to publish in what the supervisor thinks is his first year – though it is actually this third. In 'Meeting of the Minds' (Cham, 28 May 2005) student and supervisor sit opposite each other engaged in thoughts that indicate a complete lack of sympathy: the student thinks Dr Smith knows all about him and disapproves, whereas the supervisor cannot remember who he is.

Dr Smith is something of a trope: a recurring image throughout the many hundred comic strips. His lack of individuality also makes him a blank canvas that enables him to take on characteristics of other well-known tropes, each of which operates in opposition to the figure of the student. In 1999, Cham borrows from the film *The Matrix* to write a series of strips titled 'What is ... The Thesis?' Dr Smith becomes the all seeing, malevolent, yet personality-less *agent* Smith: the head of the thesis committee from whom Nerdo (our hero, here named in a nod to the character of Neo) is advised to run. In a 2005 strip, 'A Smithmas Carol' (Cham, 6 December 2005), Dr Smith is a Scrooge-like figure visited by the ghosts of students past, present and future who encourage him to mend his ways. In 'Dr Frankensmith' (Cham, 23 October 2006), he resembles the ambitious Victor Frankenstein, who uses the laboratory to create a being in his own image. Despite his malleability, each version of the supervisor contributes to an image of Dr Smith as a largely absent, patriarchal, knowledgeable and somehow disapproving figure. He is a *master* in the sense that he has the institutional position and all that this brings in terms of controlling access to the things his research students might need or want: funding, reputation, conference information and the all-important academic networks (Grant, 2008). He is also, to switch to another of Grant's frames, the *proper* traditional supervisor, with no element of the psychological supervisor, for whom supervision is an interpersonal relationship (2005). Whereas Ormerod Goode was interested in Phineas' life and health, even though Phineas himself might have preferred him to remain more traditional, Dr Smith wants to know very little about the lives of his students, even their names.

The students acknowledge Dr Smith's mastery through their inability to speak, and the dialogue between the student and supervisor is conducted through *things*, much as Grant describes: usually this thing is a piece of writing, such as a report, paper or part of the thesis (2008). In 'Meeting of the Minds' (Cham, 28 May 2005), the student is ineloquent and stammers while pointing to a diagram on a clutched piece of paper. In 'Just Call me "Dr Smith"' (Cham, 10 April 2001), the student, this time the hero's friend Mike Slackenerny, rifles through his papers saying 'Um ... hold on, Prof Smith ... I know I did some work this week'. The unnamed hero is himself often drawn clutching pieces of paper, sitting at the other side of the supervisor's desk, as he is in 'Significant Results' (Cham, 3 September 2008), or waiting outside his office in the corridor, as in 'Meeting with Advisor' (Cham, 7 August 2005).

The students in these comics are recognisably lacking in power; their subjugation is demonstrated in a number of ways, including an inability to speak to the supervisor. They procrastinate, 'I'm really not into the whole "setting goals" thing', in 'New Year's Resolutions' (Cham, 9 January 2002), and resist submitting work. When not in the supervisor's presence, Cham's students strenuously avoid it, as Cecilia does in 'Sneaking Past Advisor's Office' (Cham, 21 April 2000) or 'Hiding' (Cham, 4 March 2006). All of Manathunga's warning signs (2005) are demonstrated by Cham's research students, who are unambiguous stereotypes of unruly postgraduate research students. Conversely, they display few of the characteristics in the new (this century) skills agenda for research students. Although there is a comic strip entitled 'Transferable Skills' (Cham, 7 November 2007), it mocks the very notion, indicating that the only skill Mike Slackenerny has developed that could be useful in a 'real' job is typing. And yet, there is a degree of celebration in the unruliness of the comic's protagonists – a delight in their lack of drive and procrastination, and a playful resistance to placing value on timely completions of thesis projects or employability of graduate students.

The third type in this brief taxonomy is the *home* (here English) supervisor and the international or *foreign* student. Like Reimer's memoir, *Sandstone Gothic*, A. N. Wilson's novel *A Jealous Ghost* (2005) depicts a relationship between the UK, a significant importer of postgraduate research students, and the former settler colonies that have traditionally exported them (Pietsch, 2015). In *A Jealous Ghost*, the American Sallie arrives in London to write a PhD on Henry James' novella, *The Turn of the Screw* (1995/1998). Sallie's graduate dormitory in Bloomsbury is populated with 'African, Australian, Canadian and American seekers after abstruse knowledge and doctoral reward' (Wilson, 2005: 5). Here Wilson draws, intertextually, on the experiences of American researchers in the UK that are the subject of other British university fictions, from David Lodge's novels, Alison Lurie's *Foreign Affairs* (1984) and Byatt's *Possession* (1990). At the same time, although Wilson's novel does owe something to these twentieth-century fictional explorations of trans-Atlantic researcher exchange, it owes as much to nineteenth-century fictional accounts of Americans in England, in particular to Henry James. *A Jealous Ghost* has a strong intertextual relation to *The Turn of the Screw*, but also references James' earlier novel, serialised in 1881, *The Portrait of a Lady* (1985/1881) to underscore Sallie's experience as an American in 'old Europe' (Wilson, 2005). Sallie comes to London with a fantasy notion of what her life will be: she will be part Jamesian heroine, another innocent American abroad, and part medieval wandering scholar (or its modern-day equivalent), roaming from university to university (Wilson, 2005). Like Reimer, and like the American scholar in Lurie's novel, for whom England symbolizes *the* object of desire (Rossen, 1993), Sallie has a preconceived and somewhat idealised notion of what England will be like, gleaned from her reading of fiction.

Although it is narrated in the third person, the novel presents events from Sallie's perspective and it quickly becomes apparent in *A Jealous Ghost*, as it does in *The Biographer's Tale*, that the reader's access to the truth is limited. This narrative technique, used by Henry James, creates a distance between Sallie and the reader: we do not have access to the workings of her thoughts, and at the same time are limited to receiving an account of events solely from her distorted perspective. Oblique references to a violent past creep into the narrative, which becomes increasingly *less* typical of British university fiction in the manner of Byatt and Lodge and *more* suspenseful, in the gothic mode of Donna Tartt's *The Secret History* (1993). It also recalls *The Turn of the Screw* in which it is difficult to distinguish how much of the tale that the unnamed governess relates is the product of her own imaginative fears. It is quite apparent in Wilson's novel, however, that Sallie has a problem distinguishing between fiction and reality; the first clue comes early in the novel when Sallie assumes that her employer wants to marry her.

Sallie's ideas about what her supervisor *is* and *does* are also based on an imaginary supervisor-student relationship. Like the American literary scholars in Lodge's (1984) *Small World*, or Byatt's *Possession*, Sallie is well versed in her literary theory – unlike her English supervisor. She is *not* trying to write 'middle-brow' criticism based on biography, but is attempting to read the novel as a text about the limits of truth. She finds her supervisor's historicist reading of James' novel, his 'pedantic pencillings' in the margins of her draft chapter, and his exhortation that she be 'much' clearer about her methodology, an irritation (Wilson, 2005: 51–53). Annoyed by the practical advice of her supervisor, Sallie finds it hard to overcome the apparent difference in their approaches to James' text: where Helstone is 'historicist and realist', Sallie reads the novella through the lens of Baudrillard's concept of 'hyper-reality' (Wilson, 2005). Like *The Biographer's Tale*, Wilson's novel gestures towards a division between different paradigms within English studies, although in the case of *A Jealous Ghost*, it is the supervisor and student, rather than two supervisors, who are representative of what is figured as two different and opposing schools of thought. Eight months into the PhD, Sallie wonders if she has found what she was seeking in her supervisor, who has 'ridiculously little to contribute' (Wilson, 2005: 54). Sallie considers herself, by coming to England, to have paid a high price to do the PhD and expects something significant in return; she makes recourse to what Grant terms the discourse of Com-Supervision, in which education is reconfigured as a commodity (2005), although the price Sallie pays is not a monetary one. Sallie, unlike Cham's unnamed hero or Phineas Nanson, regards herself as a consumer of 'intellectual commodity' in the way that Knights describes (2005), although it is because she is dissatisfied, and feels that the exchange has not been fair, that she constructs the supervisory experience in this way. According to Grant (2005), the discourse of commercial supervision operates thus: it is a position that students and supervisors take up when the relationship or exchange is not going well or according to their expectations.

Interestingly, it is not emotional support that Sallie expects from her supervisor. While Sallie is unconvinced of Professor Helstone's input into her *project*, she does acknowledge his small acts of kindness to her*self*. The only English home that Sallie visits in her first eight months in England is that of her supervisor, and she does recognise that it was 'kindly meant' on his part to invite her (Wilson, 2005).

Like Phineas, Sallie does not complete her dissertation. Whereas *The Biographer's Tale* celebrates Phineas living out his two lives and writing his slippery and unreliable tale instead of his thesis (Byatt, 2000), in Wilson's gothic take on university fiction, Sallie descends into a psychotic state in which she cannot distinguish between her life and *The Turn of the Screw*, murders a child and is incarcerated in an asylum. At the novel's close, the supervisor reappears, although for the most part he is a fairly peripheral figure, having no role in Sallie's fantasy in which she lives out the governess's story. In a sense, Professor Helstone represents the reality that Sallie cannot acknowledge, and while his reading of James is satirised, his concern that Sallie's reading has little grounding in historical (or textual) actuality is finally privileged (Wilson, 2005).

Gender, power and the body in doctoral supervision

In *A Jealous Ghost*, the differences between Sallie and Professor Helstone are figured in terms of age, epistemology and cultural background, but they are also gendered: the young/female/foreign student is paired with the mature/male/English academic. Although Wilson constructs this rather conventional male-female pairing to imagine doctoral supervision (and it is important to recognise that gender is everywhere relevant, including in depictions of all male teams of researchers (Green, 2005)), he also plays with gender stereotypes rather than straightforwardly reinforcing them: *ergo*, Helstone is caring and concerned for Sallie's welfare, and Sallie murders small children in her care. On the other hand, this dichotomy reinforces a different convention in Western discourse, such as Cixous (1993) describes, that underpins the representation of Sallie as emotional, delusional and *lacking in reason*, contrasting her supervisor's sanity and reason, wisdom, and reliability. Additionally, the pairing of the young and out of place Sallie with an older, established male supervisor evokes other pedagogical relationships with the same dynamic in Western culture. Sallie is one among many representations of women students taught by male academics in popular culture, including the working-class character of Rita and her curmudgeonly, drunken tutor Frank, in the film (adapted from the play) *Educating Rita* (Russell, 1983); David Mamet's (1992) play *Oleanna*, which engages head on with complexities of power, gender and pedagogy in a one-to-one encounter in a university context; and Zadie Smith's novel *On Beauty* (2005), which pays homage to both of these texts at the same time as it reworks E. M. Forster's novel *Howard's End* (1992/1919). In all three stories, events happen behind the closed doors of the male teacher's office, that space which represents a range of pedagogical fantasies involving access and privilege, disdain and exclusion, as in Reimer's (1998) and Byatt's (2000) imaginaries, and of course *risk* (see Dawson, 2010).

As the teacher or supervisor's office is invested with meaning and association, significant shifts in the supervisor-student dynamic register when supervision is taken *out* of that space. In James Morrow's *The Philosopher's Apprentice* (2009), Mason Ambrose (the apprentice) is doing a PhD in philosophy at Hawthorne University in Boston. His first supervisor is helpful and sympathetic and they regularly meet in cafés, signalling a shift from a one-way flow of power than is traditionally depicted in representations of dyadic pedagogy. Further reversal of the male-teacher/female-student scenario is made, as Mason's supervisor is a young woman, Tracey, who is 'half in love' with Mason, as he is with her. While one implication is that theirs is a more equal relationship, signified by their place of meeting, there is also the implication that this is inappropriate and has contributed to a breach in student-supervisor relationship protocol. Another subversion of expectations occurs when Mason reveals that, rather than the two of them entering into a complicated relationship, as readers may have predicted, Tracey has a breakdown and is replaced by another supervisor, a gruff and authoritarian male. The figure of the female supervisor, Tracey, may have undermined one gender stereotype, yet she ends up conforming to another. The trope of the unstable academic woman reappears in Laura Jacobs' (2009) novel *The Bird Catcher*; Margaret Snow's supervisor, Maria Silvano, is a 'brainy' and 'bipolar' scholar who goes off her lithium, wreaks havoc at a departmental Christmas party, and has to take leave, leaving Margaret sans supervisor.

The 'half in love' syndrome in Morrow's novel recalls the 'sizzle' that Jan Parker (2009) locates in representations of student-teacher dialectics since classical times. Parker briefly charts versions of this trope in educational history, including the charisma exercised by F. R. Leavis at Cambridge in the mid-twentieth century (one that A.S. Byatt had first-hand experience of and has written about), to anecdotes about power plays in teaching, some of which are sexual, in a number of other stories, *Oleanna* included. The impact of charisma, which is as often located in the *argument* or concept as it is in the *person* (Knights, 2005; Anderson, 2009), although the two can be confused, or conflated, is a situation that seems to regularly arise in fictional dyadic relationships. Related is the idea of *eros*, or the love of philosophy, a concept which is and is not sexual love and desire (Barnacle, 2005) – Socrates, as Parker (2009) points out, often seemed to confuse the two himself. The second issue which Parker draws our attention to is that the teacher – again this is particularly relevant to doctoral supervisors – is not just transmitting disciplinary material but is actively fostering and encouraging new generations of academics. As 'disciplinary representatives' (Parker, 2009), supervisors must project an identity that inspires, enthuses and *attracts*, if doctoral pedagogy is to have a role in fostering future scholars in the discipline, as considered in Chapter 2. Additionally, the existence of the sizzle, and its perpetual return (like the uncanny) in stories depicting doctoral pedagogy, signals the challenge of upholding the old Enlightenment split that divorces the mind from the body and requires that in the university context, our House of Reason, we are not supposed to be desiring bodies, but instead be chaste minds. The regularity with which variations on the 'half in love' syndrome appears, and the presence of troublesome desire in tales of the university, signals the inability of this body/mind binary to hold. While the *manner* of the return – the reinforcement of gender stereotypes and the banal reinscription of modalities of power – is frustrating, and rather boring, as we shall see, the *fact* of its return is interesting and tells us something about the complexities of pleasure and desire in doctoral supervision.

How do these issues play out in stories of doctoral supervision in the cultural imaginary? In Rachael King's (2009) *Magpie Hall*, discussed in Chapter 1, graduate researcher Rosemary has an affair with her thesis supervisor, Hugh, an older, tenured married man. Acting on a forbidden attraction is a commonplace scenario in fiction that utilises the male-female dynamic of romance – what is significant here it that it is also linked to pedagogy. The parallels between Rosemary's own story and the nineteenth-century gothic romances she (like Sallie) studies underscore the longevity of the heteronormative romance trope: in this novel the romance genre is merged with the campus novel (a little like Byatt's *Possession*, but with less reflexivity). Rosemary is steeped in nineteenth-century romance and has swallowed, hook line and sinker, the ideal of self-fulfilment through union with another. While this is a common hope for the romance heroine, to realise the desire for wholeness through becoming (what is perhaps the ultimate Western dyad) 'man and wife' (Belsey, 1994), in this novel the union with another is also bound up with the completion of the thesis, apparent in Rosemary's fantasy (see Chapter 1) of writing with Hugh in a remote cottage to each finish their respective tomes. Hugh, the supervisor, is both a version of the unobtainable hero of heteronormative romance and closely associated with the university, in particular the

English department to which they are both affiliated. Rosemary recalls the frisson of having risky, forbidden sex with Hugh in his office – where supervision happens, behind closed doors – and laments that she has nothing to do with the rest of his life, as he has dictated. Their relationship, and its sizzle, is determined by their respective positions in the department: he is the supervisor, she is the student; he has the secure job, her position is contingent, partly on him; he has an office, a home and stability, Rosemary is itinerant, and takes all her thesis work with her in the car. Just as Mr Rochester, in Bronte's novel *Jane Eyre*, which Rosemary studies, has all the power and privilege on his side – the stately home, family name, wealth – so does Hugh. Hugh is, like Professors Goode, Smith and Helstone, *the* institution. Yet Hugh breaks the boundary of 'private' and 'pedagogical' that these other supervisors maintain by engaging in a relationship with Rosemary. Although both student and supervisor transgress this boundary, the power and the agency is stacked on one side.

Magpie Hall is one of several novels to draw on the trope of the older academic male supervisor and younger female doctoral student, and to explore that dynamic in terms of how gender and power can operate in doctoral pedagogy, in the popular imagination. In Richard Russo's *That Old Cape Magic* (2009), the narrator Griffin tells of his academic father's late-in-life dalliance with a female graduate student. Through what is represented as a series of staged seductions, Claudia, the student, attracts Griffin's father's notice and they embark on an affair, despite the university's ban on student-staff 'fraternizing'. To the caustic narrator, which becomes a blend of Griffin and his bitter mother, who is telling him the story, this ban is somewhat unnecessary, as Claudia is not after all a young undergraduate: at twenty-nine she is a grown-up who no longer needs institutional protection. What she *does* need, according to Griffin's mother, is a lot of help in completing her doctoral degree – this she gets from Griffin's father, who is depicted as falling prey to Claudia's schemes. Claudia is both wily and manipulative, and not very clever, according to the biased narrator. The story tells how Claudia and Griffin's father relocate to a cottage (recalling Rosemary's idyll) near Cape Cod, he for a year's secondment to 'UMass' and she to finish her thesis. In a twist that undermines one stereotype (female student who lacks agency) at the same time as establishing another (conniving woman), Claudia gets bored with all the writing and departs, taking her all clothes and other belongings, but leaving behind her thesis materials. According to the narrator, this is a deliberate and masterful act: the pull of the unfinished work is too much for Griffin's father, as Claudia apparently predicts, and he finishes the dissertation. The question then becomes: whose work is it? It started as something of a meeting of minds, a shared interest in the work, and the novel asks us to consider the possibility that is that not what all dissertations really are – collaborations? Yet it is officially Claudia's idea and her dissertation, as Griffin's father has already legally declared by signing off on her proposal with two colleagues. So Claudia submits the thesis, in an inversion of the popular lore that says supervisors steal intellectual property from students, reminding us that the flow of power is not one way. At the same time, and despite the fact that he has no authorship claim, Griffin's father clearly *loved* writing Claudia's dissertation. To my surprise, this aspect was something that academic readers with whom I discussed the novel reacted to, suggesting that Russo captures something of the pleasure that an academic can have in collaborating over research work despite (or because of?) it being complex and even risky to do so.

Although Claudia is cast in the role of scheming woman, who uses her sexuality to get what she wants (a finished thesis and a PhD degree), the novel undermines the veracity of this representation by calling into question *both* the narrator's intent (Griffin's mother is positively gleeful at her ex-husband's fate) *and* her sources. Apparently, she has been gleaning small nuggets of information from her various 'spies' at the university, which she stitches together into this story for Griffin, inventing what she cannot know (Russo, 2009). This tale is another version of an academic myth, in this case the affair between teacher and student, that circulate around and between campuses, each with different variations. These tales are versions of academic folk lore that offer a means of confronting or dealing with the complex and difficult, through reducing reality to trope or symbol (Burke, 1953), and by enacting a form of resistance to the dominant discourse (Zhang, 2014) or a prohibition. The prohibition is student-teacher fraternization; the discourse is that which constructs students and academics as minds without bodies, desires and emotions. What is difficult is not simply reducible to gender relations – although it is that too – but also the issue of what to *do* with the body in doctoral pedagogy.

One story of a doctoral student's *body* that is also to do with the interplay between power and gender in supervision is Byatt's novel *A Whistling Woman* (2002). The novel is set in 1968 and reflects on the radical changes for women in the mid-twentieth century, the sexual revolution that was contributed to, according to Byatt, by the widespread availability of the pill. At the start of the novel Jacqueline Winwar has nearly finished her doctoral work: with her thesis data on snails collected and the project nearly completed, Jacqueline has started to think about future plans and postdoctoral study. She decides to ask the notoriously sleazy Lyon Bowman if he will accept her as a researcher in his lab, because she wants to do precise 'hard science' on the physiognomy of memory in snails. Byatt represents Jacqueline as a serious scientist, with a strong desire to pursue difficult research work, to counter the idea, which the novel presents as prevalent at the time, that women could not be scientists because the body (sex, children, age) would get in the way. In this feminist depiction of a fictional woman scientist, Byatt shows how, for women in the 1960s, becoming a researcher was complicated and fraught as they encountered attitudes about their ability and inclination for research based on assumptions about gender taken as biological truths. Jacqueline recognises her own ambition, and while she imagines that one day she might want marriage and a family, she puts her studies – the thesis, the snails – first. Like the researchers discussed in Chapter 1, Jacqueline is perpetually in the grip of a forceful curiosity, her *desire to know* the next thing (and the next and the next) is always unmet (Byatt, 2002).

At the same time as it considers the possibility that it is possible to choose mind over body, as Jacqueline seems to, the issue of whether women and men can work together without becoming immured in sexual politics is also explored in this story. When Lyon Bowman interviews Jacqueline they play some game that is only possible, the narrator suggests, because she is a woman and he a man. He does offer her a place in his lab, but only after explaining his reservations, which include the objection that 'obsessive' women are bad for the laboratory team, and that women often leave with their work unfinished to attend to a biological imperative to have children. As it turns out, pregnancy *does* become an issue for Jacqueline who is briefly pregnant – possibly to Lyon Bowman himself, with whom she has sex one night at a conference. Although their sexual encounter *is* related to the position each holds in the laboratory – Jacqueline knows that Bowman is famous for seducing women graduate students on the promise of advancing their careers – Jacqueline is not undone by it, nor is she interested in using the power she herself potentially gains through it. Instead, their encounter at the conference is seen as a singular event, something that Jacqueline enjoyed but which does not define her or influence her actions henceforth, in keeping with Byatt's depiction of independent women and changing attitudes toward sex at the time. Research comes first for Jacqueline and neither her short-lived pregnancy nor her sexual encounter with Lyon Bowman prevent her from dedicating herself to her work, nor from being respected for it, including by Bowman, who acknowledges her tenacious and careful laboratory work with genuine respect.

While the novel does presents the possibility of reading Jacqueline's dedication to research as a choice that leads to a fulfilling and independent life, and respect from male colleagues, the scene in which she experiences the miscarriage opens another reading. The miscarriage happens while Jacqueline is at work: she rushes to the toilets where she experiences a loss of a great deal of blood and is engulfed by messy tears. She is – to paraphrase the novel – appalled by both her body, which shakes and trembles, and by her emotion, which is described as a bodily and unmanageable *thing* (Byatt, 2002). Despite

Jacqueline's best efforts to keep things neat, to separate body and mind, biology has intruded on her research domain; she has to leave, her colleagues tell her to go home, that she looks dreadful (although she manages to ask Bowman to feed the snails before she goes). Similarly, Helen Rossi in Kostova's (2009) *The Historian*, discussed in the previous chapter, also experiences a miscarriage, the day after she successfully defends her dissertation. Paul, the narrator, tells of blood on the sheets, bloody footprints on the floor, and Helen by turns worryingly quiet or in tears. Although her dissertation receives accolades, Helen, as recalled by Paul, never spoke of it again. While it is troublesome that these two twenty-first-century novels connect research success to loss and pain, as if for these women there are consequences in doing research, the mid-twentieth-century setting of both reflects the authors' interest in exploring the gender norms of an earlier era, particularly as they play out in the university. Both stories depict an intrusion of body and emotion into the scholarly (male) research realm in which doctoral pedagogy takes place, reinforcing not only that the old imaginary of a mind/body split in the university is an impossible ideal, but also that it is *always* gendered.

The stories considered here each revisit the idea of the university as a House of Reason – they remind us that men and women have bodies as well as minds, and that complexities of desire are present within doctoral pedagogy and can be difficult to disentangle from *work*. As McWilliam (2009) claims, embodied pleasure is both present in pedagogical work and important to it: students learn about a body of knowledge from a body, as Parker (2009) also argues. Yet in much of the research literature and policy on supervision, 'fleshy incursions' of either the body or emotions are to be avoided in supervision, or at least carefully managed, write Manathunga and colleagues (2013). By contrast, in their research the body and emotions are brought to the fore. Rather than avoid these elements, they argue, there is more work to do to rethink supervision, in particular the ways in which bodies fit (or not) into supervisory practices and spaces. According to their findings, dominant Western constructions of supervision *absent* bodies and spaces. I am not sure that this is true of literary and popular representations of doctoral education (which surely form part of the cultural narratives they describe), where troublesome bodies and awkward spaces are very present. In Cham's (1997f) comic, for example, the research student is *always* a body (young, sweating, anxious, trembling, clutching paper) in space (waiting outside the closed door of an office, hiding in a corridor, or sitting uncomfortably opposite the supervisor across a desk). In *fiction*, doctoral supervision is seldom the clean practice that it often is in other domains, in keeping with fiction's role to resist dominant discourse (Belsey, 1994). Rather, it is messy, emotional and physical: something quite different from the tidy pedagogical activity of institutional imaginaries.

Being part of the group: doctoral pedagogy and socialisation

The laboratory in *A Whistling Woman* depicts a jockeying for roles and projects often associated with research labs, similar to Goodman's (2009) novel *Intuition*. In a way, our ideas about the social dimensions of doctoral pedagogy are epitomised by an imaginary of the laboratory, which is, in stories about research groups like Byatt's and Goodman's, a petri dish of complex human interactions. Networking at conferences, which Byatt (2002) also represents, is another. In his account of doctoral pedagogy in the laboratory sciences, Jim Cumming (2009b) begins with an analysis of how doctoral research in labs has been represented in discourse. This, he claims, is rife with stereotypes and commonly held assumptions about the doctoral experience in this specific research context. In an earlier article, Cumming (2007) lists these assumptions as participation as a member of a group led by a supervisor; working on common problems; sharing knowledge and accessing others' knowledge, expertise and resources; conducting fieldwork or lab work; and gaining from the links of the group leader/s with industry. He terms this the 'orthodox model' of a doctoral pedagogy that is lab based (Cumming, 2007). Cumming's purpose is to demonstrate a gap between the orthodox model and *actual* practices, which he does through a fine-grained analysis of particular cases, thus questioning the accuracy of current representations of doctoral pedagogy and research in laboratory settings.

My task is a little different. My contention is that analysing how doctoral pedagogy in a laboratory setting is represented offers two potential avenues of inquiry. First, imagined labs show how doctoral pedagogy is understood as fundamentally social, and capture and convey the idea that doctoral students learn how to *be* in academia through a form of socialisation and enculturation into the discipline. The second avenue relates to the idea that PhD pedagogy occurs in a field of identification, in that expectations of students and supervisors are shaped by the images, representations and metaphorical locations of supervision that are available (Green, 2005; Manathunga *et al.*, 2013). According to this logic, imagined pedagogical sites contribute to our sense of *how things usually go* in lab groups, in the way that Taylor (2004) describes in his account of the social imaginary.

What are these representations and how do they construct doctoral pedagogyas social? The relationships and interactions between individuals within the group are a core dimension, and my initial focus; others include depictionsof material practices and setting, which I return to below. The position of the doctoral student in representations of group-based doctoral pedagogy is clearly *relational* – just as it is in depictions of dyadic doctoral pedagogy. In stories set in research laboratories, for example, there is a pecking order, with postdocs and supervisors placed above the doctoral candidate. Even at the highest levels of higher education someone has to be at the bottom, according to the promotional trailer for the film *Piled Higher and Deeper: The PhD Movie* (2011), adapted from Cham's (1997f) comic. The ones at the bottom are those who mark papers, and carry out basic research tasks – or sometimes even tasks that are not research related (see Walker *et al.*, 2008). In Goodman's (2009) novel, the lab is highly competitive, with certain allocated tasks seen as more desirable than others – because they are known to represent favour and preference from the lead researcher, and because they are a mark of acceptance, a recognition of belonging.

The motif of belonging (or not) to a research group is part of the social dimension represented in Robinson's (1994) novel *Antarctica*, the text which Green (2005) draws on to explore the idea of the doctorate as eco-social, discussed in Chapter 1. Graham, one of the scientists based in Antarctica, recalls his experience as a naïve doctoral student when he made a discovery that supported the claims of a rival group of scientists, much to the dislike of his supervisor, who then acted very coldly toward him. At first, Graham was outraged, he recalls, as he saw the supervisor's dismissal of his findings as a perversion of science, which was surely a search for the truth. He left and was ostracised, but also eventually came to see it differently, once he found and formed a group with like-minded scientists. The 'simple truth', Graham decided, was that science was *really* about making alliances – so that your argument, and the importance of it, could be conveyed. In this process of alliance-making, a researcher's own graduate students and post-docs became the closest allies of all in the 'struggle' to show, and win, the argument (Robinson, 1994). Graham became socialised into the discipline both in the sense of his induction as a doctoral student into the social dynamics, so that he understood how things usually go (Taylor, 2004), and also in terms of his (later) building of a community of closely knit scholars to support each other within the broader, combative, field.

Related, is the idea of research constellations (Hopwood, 2010; Verschueren, 2015) or clusters of doctoral and postdoctoral researchers that form around a 'star' in the field. The TV series *Bones*, discussed in the previous chapter, depicts this form of relationship-based doctoral pedagogy with Temperance Brennan, the famous researcher around whom a group of junior researchers has gathered. Pedagogical relationships of this kind are more common, although not limited to, ideas about research supervision in the sciences. Constellations form because of the reputation and status of an academic (Verschueren, 2015), which may be (particularly in the current era) based on the number and impact of publications, but there is also an element of charisma at work in the formation of constellations – the attraction of an argument or idea, or the person, or both.

86 *The idea of PhD pedagogy*

In a written account of doctoral socialisation by one of the participants in my study, there are clearly resemblances to the field of identification just described. Lillian Harris, a recently graduated PhD, outlined her idea of the doctorate in a discipline within the hard sciences. Prior to completing her PhD in Australia, she had worked as a research technician in a laboratory in NZ and her experience with this team of researchers in *this* lab fed into an imagined PhD experience characterised by community and sociability, cooperation and support:

> I went into my PhD very optimistic and full of hope that the research would be successful and propel my career forward. I thought I would be part of a community of researchers and build lifelong friendships with my fellow PhD students.
> ... When I worked in New Zealand, I had a great boss who developed and encouraged the people that worked for her. The research group was friendly and collaborative. I enjoyed working in the department, it was very social and the PhD students were supportive of each other ... I assumed that all research groups and departments would be like this. I imagined that my PhD would be similar and I would easily make friends and build my social network through the university. I thought that the lab would have other PhD students around my age and we would share the PhD experience together. I thought that I would feel like a part of the group.

However, as she then went on to describe, this was not Lillian's experience of doctoral research at all. Rather than offering a supportive research environment, together with opportunities for a sociable and friendly community life, her PhD was characterised by marginalisation and loneliness:

> I was dumped in the only office available, located next to a different lab ... Hardly anyone else talked to me during the first six months. I didn't really know what other people were working on. There were a lot of post-docs and senior research fellows, at a different stage of life to me. The other PhD students were older and many of them had kids. We were part of one department and then we became part of another department, but the lab was big enough to be self-sufficient and I didn't really feel we were part of either. I made efforts to socialise within the department, but it was hard. The new department was small and PhD students scattered in different buildings.

The office space that Lillian occupied contributed in a real and material sense to her feelings of physical isolation from the lab, and her sense of marginalisation from the research group or social site. At the same time, it also symbolises what she now remembers as abandonment: as MacLure (2003) writes, educational spaces are not *merely* places nor objective locations. Lillian's distance from the others in the lab was real, but also relational, and this is what the location came to represent in her retelling.

To reinforce her memory of extreme loneliness during the PhD, Lillian describes being unsettled in her home life outside the lab, and reports moving around a lot, seeking both a home and social groups to belong to, far away from family and friends. Earlier I considered the public/private split (sometimes a reconciliation) for the individual doctoral researcher; in a way, groups can encourage a sense of belonging or being *home* at work. Clark (2006) writes that American university fraternities and sororities resist the modern separation of public and private selves, and public and private spaces. He also considers that humanities and arts academics are more likely to confuse 'life' (outside the university) with 'work', whereas for scientists working in laboratories the separation is potentially easier (Clark, 2006). This separation was not one that Lillian could easily make, nor would have made, according to her preference: her hoped-for experience of the PhD included friendships as well as collegiality. Similarly, in Robinson's (1994) novel, Graham's research team is close: while on field trips they share tents, cooking, alcohol – they are relationships of trust, reinforcing Graham's point that getting along with one's research team, fellow-scientists, is important for one's position in the research field.

Lillian's initial doctoral imaginary was fundamentally of a *group* activity carried out by a small research community, with members supporting each other, like the orthodox science model in Cumming's (2007) analysis. The 'boss' in Lillian's first lab represents her imagined or hoped-for supervisor, someone who might both teach her and facilitate her position in the research community; in turn Lillian imagined that she might also be able to facilitate *others*' research in a similar way:

> I imagined in my new lab I would be asked occasionally to teach new students and show them techniques. I thought that they would have confidence in my abilities to teach other students. But I felt invisible. The lab was full of people with more experience.

In her initial idea of the lab, Lillian saw pedagogy as something that would flow up and down – she would learn from others and she would teach others. She described in the interview how her imagined role in the group as a teacher and facilitator was contributed to by a pamphlet sent to her by the university before she enrolled. This pamphlet suggested the PhD experience would foster *future* leaders of research groups – one day 'you'll be a group leader' too – and that junior members of the team would gradually be inducted into senior roles. This was not her experience.

Instead, her PhD took on a different pattern of relationships like the hierarchy portrayed in *PhD Comics* (Cham, 1997f): she was the doctoral student, working on a project abandoned and reassigned by the post-doc, under the umbrella of the largely absent supervisor. In Lillian's account, the dynamic between the supervisor and post-doc was not a positive one, and this negative relationship impacted on her position in the overall team and contributed to her isolation. In addition, she felt her *project* was of little interest to anyone else and did little to further the collective goals of the lab: 'I had an orphaned project. No one else was working on it. No one had worked on it in a couple of years. No one would work on it again after I left.' As Cumming's (2007) work shows, ideally, laboratory groups work on problems common to the group, and share knowledge and resources to further both the individual projects and the overall aims of the research team. An 'orphaned' project of the kind Lillian had further isolates (orphans) the doctoral researcher, as it is of little interest to the collective research team.

Lillian's third lab experience, for her post-doc, highlights the range of group dynamics in the social space of the lab. In this lab (in the UK) Lillian finally experienced what she had imagined research in a lab environment might be: well-organised groups of researchers who utilised each other's skills, functioning like a team with 'good communication'. Even so, this lab was quite competitive, which was partly due to the university having what Lillian perceived as a highly money-oriented research culture, which meant researchers felt pressure to 'get money and be producing high impact papers'. Another factor contributing to the group culture in the lab, Lillian suggests, was that it was quite male dominated, with men in lead roles who did not always get on with each other and competed for resources. At times this lead to 'friction' between the groups in the lab that Lillian did not wish to participate in, as she had strong friendships across the groups. Lillian recalls how two principal investigators of two different groups were very competitive; one had been more junior to the other but 'he was an up and comer, who up and came' and this shifted the relationship. Recalling Graham's experience (Robinson, 1994), Lillian recounts that the two men 'had differences of opinion of what was valid science and *not* valid science, and there was a lot of friction [and] really bitter rivalry [which] permeates down, because you're in that tribe'. Lillian expanded on the idea of tribes of like-minded researchers by referring to *The Big Bang Theory* television series, in which different types of researchers identify with their disciplinary group: biologists, chemists, physicists each form different 'bands'. In addition, Lillian saw the television portrayal of each group as having distinctive traits, physicists as awkward 'super-nerds' and biologists as 'social', as *accurate*. Echoing Robinson (1994), Lillian wrote of the importance of alliances with like-researchers: 'graduate students and post-docs are on your team – you need them – they're in the lab and doing the work and you need to trust them'. Often, however, the two principal investigators (PIs) would agree – for instance on what was 'bad science' or over a 'mutual enemy' – and then the interaction between the groups was smooth.

Another participant in my study, Lisa Grocott, who did a PhD in design in the USA, similarly highlighted the ways in which pedagogical relationships are to do with making alliances, and how this element is related to becoming enculturated or socialised into a discipline. Lisa gave me access to her 'playbook' in which she had written about the PhD in a series of vignettes, including one in which she describes a meeting with her advisors. Lisa's work (during her PhD and since) is interdisciplinary, which made the differences between advisors – epistemologically, methodologically – particularly apparent. The vignettes highlight that for a researcher working across more than one discipline, like those discussed at the end of Chapter 2, the issues around allying with those who may support your argument *and* the challenge of fitting oneself into a disciplinary group are complex.

> I was watching them debate their point. The philosopher was arguing that the act of designing was inherently reflective; the painter-turned-theorist was counter-arguing that designing was all about looking forward.
> It was an argument they had had before.
> I wanted to jump in and tell them the ways in which they were both right – I was the designer in the room and surely that meant I had some insights into what they were talking about. But instead I stood on the sidelines and listened as they threw quotes at each other, referencing a stream of texts I hadn't read, books I didn't want to read. I remained silent. Still. I didn't want to be shut out of the conversation. The practitioner's perspective was important, it was relevant – I wanted to join in.

The playbook and Lisa's written text (produced for my study) both highlight that forming research relationships in the PhD and developing an epistemology were intertwined, to the extent that belonging to a discipline seemed to require a form of 'blinkering', or shutting out other ideas from different sources, that Lisa was highly resistant to. Her impetus for making diverse connections was challenged by the advisors in the supervision meetings, in which each argued for their differing views and positions. As the above quote from her vignette shows, Lisa struggled at times to participate in the conversation in the literal sense (trying to speak), and in terms of being part of research conversations across different fields. Elsewhere she wrote of having to 'negate the chatter from all directions' in order to find the core of her own research work.

Lisa's attempt to *speak* is both symbolic and real, like Lillian's isolation. In both cases, Lisa and Lillian are real people with bodies, voices and emotions who inhabited real supervisory and research places, in which there are not only other bodies but also *things*. Yet those things are also meaningful and carry associations: the books Lisa hadn't read stand for her unfamiliarity with the research terrain. In fictional accounts of supervision things are what they are *and* they are meaningful: the ever-changing brand of whiskey that Phineas and Goode sup (Byatt, 2000); Rossi's porcelain cups (Kostova, 2005); the pieces of paper that Cham's (1997f) students clutch. The interactions between people and things in representations of laboratory research remind not only that research is a social practice but also that the social includes the material (Schatzki, 2002). As if to underscore this, Byatt (2002) has Jacqueline perform what Schatzki (2002) might term basic bodily actions, like pouring liquid or writing text, and she performs more complex higher order actions involving a range of bodily and cognitive tasks over time. Significantly, the relationship between bodily tasks and memory and cognition is *what Jacqueline's research is about*: how the mind is matter (Byatt, 2002). As historian Patrick Joyce (2010) reminds, we need to remember materiality in our thinking about the social, which extends to thinking about the pedagogical. We also, according to Joyce, should bring together meanings and representations *with* material and social relations – so that we do not keep reinforcing the old binaries of representation and reality, mind and body, social and material.

CHAPTER 4

The spaces of doctoral research

To gain admission was in itself, as I found, a ceremony of induction. On my first day, armed with a letter from the University of London certifying that I was a bona fide candidate for a doctorate, I was directed to a pair of huge wing doors, higher than any doors I had ever seen or indeed doors need to be. Beyond them I came upon a tall counter in elaborately carved wood. An official behind the counter, and from a considerable height, looked at me through small, steel-framed National Health glasses. To achieve that impression of superiority, he must have been sitting on a platform a foot or two above the floor.

(Reimer, 1998: 36)

My favourite bench in the nave of the old university was still being warmed by the last sun of a spring afternoon. Around me three or four students read or talked in low voices, and I felt the familiar calm of that scholar's haven soak through my bones. The great hall of the library was pierced by coloured windows, some of which looked into its reading rooms and cloister-like corridors and courtyards ... It was the end of an ordinary day; soon the sun would desert the stone tablets under my feet and plunge the world into twilight – marking a full forty-eight hours since I'd sat talking with my mentor. For now, scholarship and activity prevailed here, pushing back the verges of darkness.

(Kostova, 2005: 54)

The spaces that doctoral researchers inhabit in the cultural imaginary of the PhD signify ideas about the nature and purpose of a higher education. Arguably, cultural practices have engaged *more* than other strands of discourse in reflecting on the meanings of the spatial dimensions of the university; just think of how many representations there are in film and television of university campuses and what associations with knowledge, culture, learning, socialisation and privilege they carry. Making a similar point, Philip Temple (2014) writes that the task of considering universities in spatial terms has until recently fallen to writers of fiction and poetry, who are not afraid to evoke a university setting through imagery and other poetic means. Angela Brew (2001) acknowledges this capacity by opening *The Nature of Research* with a fictional vignette in an evocative academic setting that thrums with tranquillity and contemplation, inquiry and collection. Writers know that spaces are connotative, and that university buildings draw on and produce cultural associations and ideas about higher education. This chapter examines these ideas and the connections between the imagined spatiality of the university and ideas of its purpose, specifically in terms of the PhD. Who are the doctoral students that inhabit the university, and what is the nature of the academic work they do in the cultural imaginary of the PhD? The chapter furthers the concerns of previous chapters by revisiting ideas of research, researchers, pedagogy and sociality in terms of *space*.

One way in which the spatial elements of a university connect to an idea of its purpose is through its design, as this chapter considers. University architecture gives deliberate expression to the ideals of an institution and university sites can be *read* to identify ideologies that underpin their construction (Ossa-Richardson, 2014; Whyte, 2015). To paraphrase Rothblatt (1997), every campus has a story to tell. One way to read a campus is through critical analysis of the design of individual buildings which incarnate an idea – as in the twenty-first-century 'information commons' that Gulson and Symes (2007) discuss, or the 'business school' Sturm and Turner (2011) critique. Another way is through reading the design of an entire campus, which expresses an idea of or ambition for a university, such as in the planned university campuses of nineteenth-century North America (Rothblatt, 1997; Gumprecht, 2007) or mid-twentieth-century Britain. In his interpretation of the latter, Anthony Ossa-Richardson (2014) traces the ideological underpinnings of campus design at Sussex, East Anglia and York: each campus is read for its concrete (Ossa-Richardson's pun) manifestation of ideas of the university as a community of scholars, as broadly socialist, or as promoting the self-development of an individual. Notably, the campuses do not necessarily embody a singular idea; rather, they bear traces of differing ideas about the nature of a university, historical and contemporaneous. Similarly, in a recent Chinese university discussed by Zhang (2014), the design is underpinned by several discourses: of rationality (evident in the grid and linear design), of consumerism (as displayed by the spread of roads with tariffs) and of fast and 'aggressive' change (evident in the way the campus is frequently reconfigured). It perhaps goes without saying that *represented* campus spaces and buildings also signify ideas about the university through their imagined design.

If campus design (real or fictional) tells us something about the ideologies underpinning an institution, the stories that circulate around and about university campuses reveal how it is imaginatively *lived* by students and academics. In the Chinese university, as Zhang (2014) demonstrates, students reconceptualise and reclaim the university space as individually experienced (by eating legendary chicken drums), imagined (with hauntings and other uncanny events), and as having a history (through stories handed down by generations of students). Our relationship to a place is complex, as Zhang's (2014) example shows, and involves personal and social history, memory and imagination. According to Somerville (2010), places are invested with meanings that are both individual and collective: stories about place can be condensed cultural narratives, as Somerville suggests, but they are also reshaped by the individual lived experience. My sense is that individuals' stories about universities, like those of the PhD participants in my study, draw on inherited cultural myths, their lived experience, and their imagination and memory as part of a process of engaging meaningfully with a place which is *being* a PhD. I draw on ideas about spatiality and dwelling from writers such as Bachelard (1994), Lefebvre (1991/1974) and Heidegger (1971/1954) here, but also an account by Siegel (1981) of Cornell University's campus and its myths. Siegel shows how the setting of the university, its relation to the gorge, graveyard and town, connects with an idea about what constitutes academic work, which in turn affects the 'imaginative scenario' of being a student or academic in that place.

Cultural narratives and representations of the university are often inflected with a sense of longevity and tradition, even nostalgia. In film and fiction, a quite specific ancient university setting is evoked through depictions of park-like grounds, stone edifices and cloistered walks: a variation on the Oxbridge ideal. In the film *Educating Rita* (1983), the newly arrived working-class student Rita walks through this kind of tranquil environment in search of her tutor's office; from his window, she looks down on the students resting on the green below, and envies their capacity to belong to the place. Literary representations of higher education have long drawn on an idea of an elite university that excludes the would-be student through their depictions of stone towers and spires. In Thomas Hardy's *Jude the Obscure* (1985/1895), the spires of the university in far-off Christminster are an image of Jude's aspiration and desire for learning, but also his class-based exclusion. For Evelyn Waugh's Charles Ryder in *Brideshead Revisited* (2009/1943), made into a popular TV series in the 1980s, the 'dreaming spires' represent not only the place of Oxford (and something like Jude's privilege, from the inside) but also another time: his nostalgia for an Oxford of the past, his own youthful affections and sexual experiences, and the beauty and innocence of his life before the horrors of the Second World War. More recent representations of the university continue this tradition. For colonial PhD student Reimer (1998), the spires of Oxford represented the hallowed centre of British learning and culture, from which he, as an Australian, seemed particularly distanced. The poem 'The Hopwood doctorate' (Retana, 1998) draws on these associations, in particular architectural motifs of privilege/exclusion, to convey what it means to be a Chicano PhD student in a prestigious North American university on the cusp of the twenty-first century: like Rita, the speaker walks through the campus feeling simultaneously belonging (having a right to be there) *and* being out of place.

Architectural metaphors like Oxford's spires are utilised in cultural imaginaries of the PhD to convey ideas of the university and its purpose. A tower (particularly an ivory one) signals both the idea of the university as removed from the rest of society, and the separation of disciplines in the nineteenth century (Standaert, 2014, Collini, 2008). In A. S. Byatt's tetralogy of novels that includes *Babel Tower* and *A Whistling Woman* there are towers for each discipline: language, evolution, mathematics and social sciences (Byatt, 1996). Cloisters, on the other hand, represent both a monastic removal of the university from the rest of society *and* communal or collective aspects of the institution. In Byatt's (2002) novel Jacqueline Winwar conducts her research at York in the 1960s which, like the actual campus in Ossa-Richardson's (2014) account, has connecting walkways that link the various towers and resembles a beehive (Byatt, 1996). As Jacqueline's own research is cross-disciplinary, linking the study of memory to the study of 'matter', it is suited to the space. In this particular university imaginary, realised in the actual York campus, encounters between the disciplines and between researchers, even incidental ones, as Ossa-Richardson (2014) outlines, are fostered. In this idea of the university research is an individual *and* collective endeavour: each member of the university works toward the common ideal and the pursuit of knowledge.

A philanthropist's dream: the idea of the PhD in a North American campus

Any idea that has a long history, like the idea of the university, will carry long-held perceptions into contemporary understandings and local iterations. Arguably, there has been one idea of the university – one that situates the individual in his or her setting quite decisively – which has been particularly influential on a cultural imaginary of the university and on campus design. We are of course back with Cardinal Newman. Many of our present-day associations with university spaces are contributed to, directly and indirectly, by Newman's (1871) mid-nineteenth-century writings in which he links an idea of the university firmly to place – in fact a particular place. Newman's experiences of, and attachment to, the ancient Oxford quadrangles coloured his idea of the nature and purpose of a university. For Newman, a liberal education involved living *in* college, with all that that meant for being in that environment, breathing in the air, soaking up the intellectual traditions, and forming friendships. Even Newman's idea of how learning happens is informed by his affection for Oxford and its spatial character: knowledge is *absorbed* by students simply by living there and being part of an ancient tradition of learning. According to Rothblatt (1997), Newman drew on mid-nineteenth-century ideas which informed the way university spaces were understood, one being the idea of the *genius loci*, the god in the grove or spirit inhabiting a place (an idea Romantic poets and landscape gardeners were also fond of). Newman's description of a student learning through atmosphere and tradition, independent of particular teachers, is informed by a sense that a non-corporeal force, inherent in the place because of its long history, can exert influence. A contemporary explanation for this phenomenon comes from Joyce (2010), who suggests that university infrastructure has a pedagogical function: the liberal subjects are *shaped by* the material things around them. Cloisters and quadrangles, according to this idea, exert agency.

A related idea informing understandings of university spaces in Newman's day, and which continues to influence contemporary university design, is what Rothblatt (1997) terms associationism. Associations are fostered by the design of particular symbols or structures (a stairway, a window, a tower or quadrangle) which refer to the continued influence of the past and the long history and tradition of universities like Oxford or Cambridge. These architectural structures are recycled in, and borrowed by, newer institutions, or by colonial institutions (Pietsch, 2013), to evoke and carry on long-held traditions of an ancient university, shore up their own status *as* a university, and contribute to an idea of 'the university' that transcends particular institutions (Pietsch, 2013; Whyte, 2015). Associationism, writes Rothblatt (1997), was the ideal theory for the boom decades of the university in the nineteenth century because it helped justify the juxtaposition of old and new buildings, as well as the recycling of 'old' styles in the 'new' civic universities from the middle of the century. This association did not always work to the new universities' advantage, however. Whyte (2015) suggests that the tendency of new universities to recycle architectural styles (cloisters and quadrangles) contributed to redbrick institutions being dismissed merely as poor imitators of Oxbridge.

The collegiate setting that Newman so admired, and which was important to his idea of the liberal education of an individual, was transported to North America and influenced the design of the campuses there, albeit with a degree of variation. Rothblatt (1997, 2006) outlines how the American campuses, starting with Harvard, borrowed from Britain the secluded and enclosed form of the university college but modified and adapted it by loosening the quadrangle into an open collection of buildings that better reflected American ideals of democratic individualism. According to Rothblatt, American colleges 'tore down' the walls that separated the institutions from their surroundings and opened the campus to the wider public in a 'democratic gesture' – and an antidote to the old-world gown *vs.* town idea (Rothblatt, 1997). It seems fitting now to consider these ideas in terms of the cultural imaginary and a narrative about doctoral study set in one such North American campus.

In Michael Collins' *The Secret Life of E. Robert Pendleton* (2006), graduate student Adi Wiltshire attends an American college, the fictional university of Bannockburn founded in the early twentieth century, following a bequest from a wealthy industrialist, Iosif Zhvanetsky. The college was built on the site of a former clothing factory. The site is significant for several reasons. It is located on the bend of a river on a piece of land which became an island when the factory owner, described as an illiterate Russian émigré, dug away the slim piece of remaining land in a pseudo-feudal gesture. The factory was destroyed by a fire in 1911, killing eighteen women workers who had been locked inside. The industrialist was both rich and remorseful, and made provisions for his wealth to be used to establish a women's college on the factory ruins following his death. After a series of highs and lows, engendered partly by the events of the twentieth century, the university settled in 1952 into its permanent incarnation as a small co-ed liberal arts college, a 'venerable cradle of learning' (Collins, 2006: 4–5). The location and the history of Bannockburn are entwined: it was founded, like many American universities, including Cornell (Siegel, 1981), by a philanthropist. Its particular history is thus tied not only to the manufacturer's posthumous generosity, like Ezra Cornell's, but also to his greed, his guilt over the negligence that resulted from it, and his unrequited love for a woman worker who died in the fire. Ostensibly a monument to a story of success and the American dream, the college can also be seen as founded on rank materialism at its most selfish and destructive, and on death. By the time Adi does her PhD in the 1980s, the factory is part of the institution's repressed history: the site of the original factory has been purposely left to turn to a wilderness. If universities contain a god in the grove to animate their purpose, what spirit dwells in such a place, and what is its influence on the university and the people who work in it? This question is at the heart of this novel.

The grim origins of Bannockburn are retold and elaborated through campus myths and tales of hauntings in the wilderness area. One story purports that the bones of the Russian manufacturer's parents are interred beneath the small house in which he grew up, a house that he had transported from communist Russia and rebuilt on the college grounds to stand in homage to 'peasants' who had made their mark on the world. Bannockburn's stories and origins underscore its associations with Cornell University, which was founded, according to Siegel (1981), out of Ezra Cornell's awareness and/or refusal of his own mortality following a period of illness, coupled with his desire to help other similarly humble men rise to better fortune, an ideal shared by many North American universities (Retana, 1998). The choice of the university's location was because of the view, which had 'something' to do with death (Siegel, 1981). These associations continue as part of the idea of Cornell and how its inhabitants imagine themselves in relation to it, partly because of its location in relation to the graveyard, the nearby gorge and the town (Siegel, 1981). In the case of Bannockburn, the location is associated with the founder's success, desire and greed, and with violent death – that turn out to be the themes central to Collins' novel, which is both campus fiction in the satirical vein, with ambitious and competitive academics, and a crime novel that ties (once again) the search for truth about an unsolved crime to ideas about doctoral research as discovery – in this case the discovery of a hitherto unknown manuscript.

The location of the campus on an island (albeit a man-made one) is also meaningful, as it endows the college with the capacity to disengage and isolate itself from the mainland by cutting off the one access road. Frequent references are made in the text to the college's enclosed physical status, close to, but also separate from, the nearby town, a quintessential image of the college's liberalism (Collins, 2006). Again, there are associations with Cornell, which was built within easy distance of, yet separate from, the nearby town (Siegel, 1981). Like Bannockburn, Cornell's isolation was for a long time physically reinforced by the gorge which runs close to the campus, requiring any visitors to traverse over a precarious-seeming bridge. This positioning reinforced an idea of the campus, and the imaginary scenario in which *research* happens (Siegel, 1981), summarised by Derrida (2004/1983) as being to do with expansion and enclosure. For Bannockburn's inhabitants, *inside* the college represents a place of safety, a 'cocoon' of isolation rarely infiltrated by life outside (Collins, 2006). Being allowed *in* is an indicator of the liberal ethos and a mark of individual achievement. Visiting academic Horowitz recognises this when he visits Bannockburn and notices the floodlit student car park, keeping the dark at bay, which is filled with expensive cars. This contrasts to the 'slum' he grew up in and reinforces his distance from that past: he has 'made it' and what's more he has *achieved it by himself* (Collins, 2006). After all, merit and opportunity are equal, are they not? (Retana, 1998). For the inhabitants of the town, descendants of the families whose histories mirror the those of the founding-father, yet who have since fallen on hard times due to a waning regional economy, the college is inaccessible, a place for privileged students from *elsewhere* to attend. Ex-Vietnam veteran Wright, who has returned to study for his Bachelor of Arts (he never shortens it to BA, we are told) as a part-time mature student, points out that no-one from his class at the local high school came to the college, that no-one from the town has 'made it' as Horowitz has.

Like the college's academics, Adi is not a local. Collins (2006) represents Adi as a child of nomadic academic parents who were immersed in the counter-culture of the 1960s (whose own doctorates remain unfinished), and for whom the college and its architecture represent something permanent and lasting, contrasted against the transitory nature of her life. Bannockburn's solidity and isolation are compared to the state college in Ohio where Adi's parents had been to school, and where she had been born and raised in an era of 'free love' and peaceful protest. Her parents are described as having been idealistic graduate students who had wanted to change the world and make it a better place. By contrast, Bannockburn has neither an American state school's egalitarian principles nor its campus design.

Although Adi admires the ivy-covered buildings as representative of the institution's longevity, and the stability she craves, the architecture of the Bannockburn campus is less Ivy-League and more of a mishmash of various university architectural memes in a form of associationism gone wild. These include the traditional manicured quad, lead-panelled stained glass and polished oak doors (Collins, 2006). The novel self-consciously presents this anachronistic architectural muddle to show how a range of ideas about the university and its purpose are brought together. In one scene, Collins (2006) juxtaposes two buildings to portray different ideas about knowledge and education from different times: the Earth Sciences 'legacy' building and the new library. While the library is characterised by concrete and openness, the older building has a cathedral-like vaulted ceiling with neogothic flying buttresses and a marble floor. The older building is connotative of the transition from the founder's former 'peasant' life to wealth, but also of the idea of eternal reward through its borrowing from church design. At the same time, the narrator tells us, this building represents a 'secular shrine' to knowledge and learning. Within the grand atrium is a small statue of the college's philanthropist, a humble figure, beneath which is a statement valorising the nineteenth century ideal of 'success through industry'. The atrium and the plaque pay homage to the man and an idea: the liberal ethos that a university education can elevate an individual to a higher status, whether it be via transcendental knowledge (as Adi contemplates) or material wealth, or both (Collins, 2006: 259–260).

As a researcher, Adi is initially a generalist: the product of a liberal education. Although widely read, she has no real focus, which is problematic for a PhD. A series of events, including the attempted suicide of academic and writer Bob Pendleton, leads her to his archive of materials, including an unreleased manuscript revealing details of an unsolved murder. With this find, Adi has a focus, a thesis and a specialism, and at the end of the novel she too has fulfilled the Bannockburn dream of individual achievement and has completed her thesis to acclaim, has a tenured teaching position (elsewhere) and becomes distinguished as a Pendleton scholar. Even so, Adi undergoes several setbacks before her thesis is completed, including a period in which she experiences knowing the indeterminacy of research, that there were no answers, no real truth, which includes not ever *really* knowing what Pendleton's involvement in the murder had been. The realisation of not knowing, not solving the clues to the murder, momentarily undermines Adi and recalls her parents' research failures all too acutely. They too had research goals that were idealistic, but finally came to nothing. In her mother's case, this lead to a departure from graduate student counter-culture and a turn toward the comforts of wealth and materialism. In a sense, Adi is the ideological offspring of the collapsed optimism of the radical era, and a belief in the possibilities of research as a means of bringing about societal change, both of which are represented by state education and its incarnation in the Ohio campus complex of her childhood. Finally, although she worries about it, in the end Adi chooses to accept that indeterminacy in research is inevitable, and that she might as well reap the material benefits and status that accrue because of what she has discovered, however shaky its integrity may be.

In the closing section of the novel (entitled 'Indeterminacy'), Adi sends Horowitz to the concrete library to retrieve her controversial, dangerous and therefore hidden thesis. He finds the thesis disk on the eighth floor, where Adi has tucked it into a work transcribed in the Dark Ages by monastic scholarly monks, a time when 'Western civilisation' retreated to remote islands to protect Knowledge (Collins, 2006). The image of a hidden repository of knowledge, protected by the forebears of academic scholars attempting to hold back the tide of ignorance and savagery, is an enduring one in cultural representations of doctoral work, including *The Historian*, discussed in Chapter 1. The usual function of this image is to underscore an idea of the university as preserving and protecting knowledge, keeping the flame of Western scholarship. However, it does not function *here* in quite that way, for what Adi has achieved in her doctorate is not a contribution to knowledge in the sense that she initially imagined or hoped. By the end of the novel, she is quite self-consciously a sell-out, an academic who has given up on her youthful ideals in order to claim academic success and status of a worldlier variety. No-one in this satire is that imagined 'real thing', the academic who has as his or her goal transcendental knowledge, or social change. And so the spaces of this institution, the novel seems to imply, are also inauthentic, mere mimicry of an ideal university, not the thing itself.

The library and the archive: a small safe place

There are few spaces as evocative of hidden or protected knowledge as a library, as Collins' (2006) novel indicates. Likewise, with the possible exception of the scientist in a laboratory, there are few images that evoke *research* as strongly as a scholar entering into the archive, anticipating the find that lies in its dusty embrace. In the last century, Derrida (1995) termed the Western predilection for archival research in the humanities as 'archive fever'. Certainly, the archive seems to have a strong allure for researchers in its promise of connection with a bygone time and the possibility of discovering truth. Despite the radical shifts, since the end of the last century, towards archival matter becoming open access (McGann, 2007; Folsom, 2007), as textual archives become increasingly accessible online and without the restrictions of old, the image of the researcher *gaining access* to an archive is a central trope of the imagined research student reproduced in the cultural imagination across a wide variety of genres and practices, and reimagined and retold by individual PhD researchers. This particular imagined research space contributes to a conceptualisation of doctoral research that is tied up with notions of status and privilege, safety and belonging, and authenticity (or being) in the place of research. It is also tied to a particular imaginary of the university in which the *book* is central.

Entry to the archive in a library, public record office or museum represents a rite of passage, when the researcher, who, as discussed in Chapter 2, is often a marginal figure not (yet) fully an academic, is issued with an access card and can enter that privileged space that he or she has joined – a small select group with its own rules and associated rituals of showing an access card, donning gloves, finding the right carrel. Historian Harriet Bradley (1999) recalls, at the turn of the twenty-first century, her initiation into archival research as a doctoral researcher seventeen years earlier. Elements of the trope of an encounter with the archives which are the focus of this section are all present in Bradley's account. She alludes to the pursuit for original findings; the 'thrill' of gaining access or being allowed 'in' to join a select or privileged cohort, and of engaging in activities, practices or rituals associated with that group; being inside the space of the archive, often characterised as highly imposing on the outside yet safe and light within; and encounters with objects in the space, including favoured desks and old, large, leather-bound books. Bradley describes being inside the walls of the Bodleian or the British Museum as a safe place or place of retreat from the competitive world of academia, protected from attack and at the 'heart of her craft' (Bradley, 1999). Bradley's memory of the archive draws on her lived experience and engages what Lefebvre terms representational space, or physical space that is changed and appropriated by the imagination which makes symbolic use of its objects (Lefebvre, 1991/1974). In this way, the imposing frontage, the large books and the old desks carry associations with research – even as they are real *things*. At the same time, this memory of becoming a researcher through doctoral study also constructs the archive as what Bachelard (1994/1958) terms a felicitous space, or space that is loved.

Entry to the archives is a moment that marks not only the beginning of a new way of life, but also an initiation into a long-established form of scholarship. One participant in my study, Ian Brailsford (PhD, History), travelled from NZ to the USA to do archival work and wrote of a moment when he realised that he was *there*: 'The end of my first real week in the American archives. Sitting in the landscaped gardens of Duke University in North Carolina at lunchtime on the Friday of a very hot July day. Thinking "This is it, I'm really doing my doctorate now."' Bronwyn Lloyd (PhD, English and Art History), described in her written imagining her first encounter with/in an archive.

> The main activity that I was involved in during the first year of my doctoral research was transcribing the archive of letters [approx. 400, written from the 1940s to late 1960s (int.)]. The National Library was then fairly low-tech, and visitors could only use pencils to take notes, or pay exorbitant charges to have the librarians photocopy material for you. This low-tech style of research perfectly suited the nature of my doctoral study.
>
> I arrived at the Library each morning and made my way upstairs to the issues desk where the files of correspondence I had ordered the previous day were waiting for me. Gathering a few sharpened pencils from the container at the edge of the desk, I entered the low-lit research room where I would sit and transcribe the letters, noting in the margins of my notebooks all the things I needed to investigate further. Occasionally, other researchers were present, immersed in their own projects, but more often than not I was alone in the room with Rita Angus's letters.
>
> The abiding image I have is of the dim light and long table in the reading room at the Alexander Turnbull Library [an annex to the national library], and of the route I took up Molesworth Street each afternoon on my short walk home to the flat in Thorndon that I shared with my sister. On sunny afternoons, I would walk through the botanical gardens, have coffee in Thorndon Village, and then take a stroll past Rita Angus and Douglas Lilburn's former homes in Sydney Street and Ascot Terrace. Walking past their houses, I experienced the strange sensation that I was an active participant in the story of their lives – a story that was still going on after their deaths.

Access to the archives felt like a privilege to Bronwyn, as she was allowed in to the space where protected matter is housed; the access was also hard-won, as initially she was denied entry by the Angus estate. Access *should* be hard, as Rothblatt (2006) considers in his account of universities as utopias, and the thrill of entry to the difficult or obscure place is a necessary precursor to gaining new knowledge, which leads to enlightenment.

Physical elements of Bronwyn's archival space also have, as Lefebvre suggests, symbolic meaning: the dim light, long tables, the quiet, the pencils and notebooks for transcribing are all evocative of monastic study. (Brew (2001) employs similar imagery in her depiction of the archive, representing the idea of research as scholarship.) Bronwyn also describes a sense of the intimacy (another kind of privilege) afforded by the act of reading alone the 'deeply private' letters of Rita Angus to Douglas Lilburn, the kind of intimacy of working with textual remains that Carolyn Steedman describes (2001) in her account of archival work.

> My imagination was fed by the knowledge that as I examined each of the letters, I was as close as it is possible to get to inhabiting the heart and mind of another person. The sense of excitement I felt in knowing that Rita Angus's hands had touched these pages, and that her feelings and beliefs flowed through the nib of her pen onto the paper, never diminished. At no point did I take for granted the privileged position I found myself in, having been granted permission by the Angus Estate to view the artist's deeply private letters to the man she loved.

The materiality of the letters and the place are part of the archive's appeal to Bronwyn's imagination. For despite the possibilities for democratised scholarship that open access of online archive allows, the physical archive has a firm hold on the imagination. As Ed Folsom has written, archives are all about the physical experience, such is their allure for researchers (Folsom, 2007). This has a lot to do with notions of authenticity or *being there* articulated over and over in cultural constructions of research, and by participants in my study who do archival work: to *touch* the page, or *be* in the place where historical matter is housed.

An experience of archival wonder is fictionalised in Lloyd Jones' *Mr Pip* (2006), when research student Mathilda, who grew up on an island in the Pacific and in Australia, arrives in London to do research in the British Library's Reading Room for her thesis on *Dickens' Orphans*. Mathilda remarks on the fact that she has joined the ranks of scholars working on Dickens, yet is self-conscious about coming from a small island in the Pacific and worries about her outsider status, that she does not really belong. Like other colonial research students, Andrew Reimer (1998) is one, Mathilda is worried that she may be denied entry to the library. This novel draws on a long history of university exclusion in its depiction of Mathilda's entry to the archive. A famous example of being shut out of a library comes of course from Virginia Woolf (1989/1929). Feminist literary scholar Susan Hardy Aikin (1986) considered the well-garrisoned library in Woolf's text a synecdoche for Western academia which allowed entry to a privileged few: Oxford's Bodleian epitomises the jealously guarded property (knowledge) of the mid-Victorian male. Although Aikin primarily discusses the exclusion of *women* from the academy, the same history that Isabel, the research assistant, acknowledges in her written imaginary, in Chapter 1, there were (and are) rules about who can enter research libraries and archives and who cannot.

Due to the existence of rules regarding entry, and the guardians who enforce them, the routine of handing over the piece of paper that proves eligibility and enables entry has symbolic meaning, particularly for those traditionally marginalised from higher education. For Roland Michell in *Possession* (Byatt, 1990), the pleasure of entering the Reading Room at the London Library arises partly because he is so conscious of his working-class origins and the traditional prohibitions against entry based on class (the Jude syndrome). Australian Andrew Reimer (1998) recalls *his* first admission to the British Museum Reading Room in *Sandstone Gothic*, underscoring the necessity of possessing proof of legitimate status: his letter from the University of London certifies his status as a 'bona fide' doctoral student. Reimer recalls in detail the rituals of entry he underwent, and the *things* both symbolic and real that were associated with these rituals, as well as the sense of being intimidated by the guard who had the power to bestow or deny access.

The imposing design of the edifices of archives and museums adds to their intimidation *and* sense of privilege for a new researcher, just as the manicured garden do in Retana's (1998) poem. The architectural qualities of British research sites like the Bodleian Library in Oxford (Bradley, 1999), the Reading Room at the British Museum and the British Library have significance in the cultural imagination, and appear frequently in novels, memoirs and other imaginings (Lodge, 2010/1965; Byatt, 1990; Reimer, 1998; Jones, 2006; Niffenegger, 2009). One participant, Jessica Daniels (PhD, Art History), wrote of the importance of institutions like libraries and archives to her idea of PhD research, and makes particular mention of the design of the National Art Library at the Victorian and Albert Museum in London, which held strong associations:

> It is a late 19th century building, but built to resemble an Italianate Renaissance palazzo. It is a little rundown, but the veneer of age and scholarship makes it seem quite regal. I did my MA in London and found

it a wonderful place to study. Particularly on fine days, with the sun streaming in the windows and the view across the courtyard, it somehow felt like you were transported to another time and place. Words and phrases that come to mind are: serious, stillness, focus, hushed quiet, the studious sounds of people making notes with pencils or gently tapping on laptop keys. Golden light streaming in windows, catching dust motes, but stately and scholarly. Feeling the long history of scholarship both being practices in the room and held within its collection.

One effect of an imposing or regal frontage is that, once access is gained, the researcher feels protected or 'held'. Inside, the researcher is cocooned by the very mechanisms – the architecture, librarians and guards – that made entry difficult. From the *outside* the library is a daunting prospect; *inside* it is a different matter, and everything associated with that interior, the objects and the light, become familiar and evocative of scholarship.

In many stories about archives there is often a very specific, particular place associated with doing research: a favourite seat. In Gowers' (2009) novel, discussed in Chapter 1, Kit spends a lot of time in the Bodleian researching Dickens in the upper reading room, where she has a favourite spot: there, she feels calm, warm, peaceful and enclosed, a feeling that is enhanced by the sight of night falling outside. Diana Bishop (Harkness, 2011) has occupied the same preferred spot since her doctoral student days in the Bodleian, which had always been 'a sanctuary' and where her chosen seat faces the gothic windows. The favourite seat is often jealously guarded, as Bradley (1999) describes, because it represents safety, familiarity and retreat. In these stories, the research space, the archive, steadily shrinks from the large imposing exterior to the friendly interior, to the small safe place that is the researcher's very own, a single chair or bench with a desk. The further in the researcher gets, the more private and secure the space becomes, the more one's own. In *The Historian* (Kostova, 2005), Paul heads to the library to study, alone and undisturbed, in monastic silence. Paul also has a favourite spot and a familiar routine. Like Isabel, as discussed in Chapter 1, Paul notices the shift from the dark *outside* the library to the feeling of light, warmth and peace *inside*. The motif is of a protected, felicitous (Bachelard, 1994/1958), and cosy space in which the small safe place of the archive contrasts to the world outside, which is peopled with all kinds of creatures who are quite malevolent (there are always things that go bump in the night, in Oxford, according to Harkness (2011)). This is not quite the 'cut-throat' world of academia that Bradley (1999) refers to; rather, the Oxford of these novels draws heavily on the tradition of crime and mystery writing set in the university and surrounding city (Earwaker and Becker, 2002) which is, potentially, far more threatening.

Crucially, it is *light* that demarcates the boundary of the small safe place. In Jessica's account of the National Art Library above, the space and light contribute to a sense of the long history of scholarship. Another participant, A. K. (PhD, English Literature), also wrote about the importance of light to an idea of research work: 'if a space is evocative for me of that kind of engagement with literature, it would be a room that was simultaneously shady and luminous.' In particular, for A. K., a sense that she was engaged in scholarship was contributed to by 'working at the Bender Room at the top of the Stanford Library in summer evenings, when it was suffused with a golden light and looking out at the hills.' In stories about archives in literary and popular culture, light is likewise soft and tempered, in order to protect delicate old books and manuscripts: not too bright, or too dark, notes Mathilda (Jones, 2006). This gentle golden light is also figurative, metonymically linked to, and standing in for, a tradition of learning and scholarship. As Derrida (1982/1972) outlines, there is a persistent figuring of *light for truth* in Western philosophy. Knowledge, reason and learning keep the darkness of ignorance, violence and superstition at bay, as Paul hopes in Kostova's (2005) novel, and as Horowitz imagines in Collins' (2006) novel. Light is truth: we know this from a long tradition in Western culture.

Yet even as the research space is characterised by light in the cultural imaginary of the PhD, there are often reminders that somewhere, in the depths of the building or institution, there are places where no light reaches. While on the one hand a vast accumulation of ancient texts can be reassuring, testament to Western enlightenment, the sheer scale of an archive like the Bodleian's collection can also be figured as overwhelming, the depths of the library collection unfathomable, like knowledge itself, or even destabilising in that it threatens to exceed categorisation. In Brew's (2001) fictional vignette depicting scholarship, the archive is dark and musty, the imagery denotes a heavy, stilted and airless place in which time seems to have stopped and *life* is excluded. The researcher, Charles, notes 'piles of decaying documents' and 'brown-ness' (Brew, 2001: 30–31). Hints of the vast subterranean collection at Oxford appear in Harkness' (2011) novel and are less evocative of illuminating dimensions of knowledge than decay; when Diana finishes with the ancient book she sends it back to the stacks, into the 'bowels of the library'. At odds with the light and airiness of the gothic windows, which point up toward the sun and heaven, are the regions of the archive's lower reaches, where vast numbers of books and manuscripts, far more than those on display, are kept. Again, this is a familiar trope: the stacks in the British Library are also referred to as its bowels in Jones' (2006) novel, and in Byatt's (1990) *Possession*, Roland visits the British Museum in search of his supervisor, who works 'in the bowels' of the museum. It is not exactly a great leap to go from 'bowels' to excrement, and Byatt follows the association to its logical end and take us there: the lower floors of the museum smell like 'tom-cat', and Roland's supervisor James Blackadder works with the 'leavings' of the Victorian poet he studies.

Although archival matter is not always referred to in *quite* such evocative terms, the association with dust is nonetheless very present in many depictions of archival research. Brew's (2001) description of the archive *opens* with the word 'dust', which lies like a blanket over the decaying books and documents. The librarian who handles the manuscripts requested by Diana Bishop has traces of rusty dirt from the old leather bindings on his woollen jumper, and Diana resists the urge to wipe her hands after touching it; when she gets back to her college rooms after a day at the Bodleian, she changes out of her grimy clothes, wondering how she got so filthy in a library (Harkness, 2011). In Grossman's (2012) novel *Codex*, the researcher-detectives Margaret and Edward search through the library's subterranean stacks which are, in contrast to the modern and well-lit 'glacial' library above, a vast dark and grimy space, a 'dark forest' of 'uncatalogued materials' in which the researchers get lost, with books and objects all covered in 'drifts of silent dust'. Historian Carolyn Steedman, in *Dust* (2001), muses on the meaning of archive fever as a (literally) feverish response to spending time cooped up with the matter of the dead that comes on at night, after a day in enclosed in dusty archives. Steedman moves across several meanings of dust in the archive: from the dust that lingers in material form on the texts of the past; to the tiny 'flotsam' or dust-like trace that is the small piece of evidence relevant to one's research found in the great heaps of textual evidence; to the *actual dust* produced by nineteenth-century industrial processes of the textile industry, including book production. The smell of old books, the dust, or even red rot, are the stuff of a scholar's life (Steedman, 2001).

Archival dust, a consciousness about its origins, and a recognition of its potential to be unhealthy for a researcher (an unfortunate side-effect of archival work), recur repeatedly in stories of graduate work in the archive. One explanation is indicated by the terms *work* or *labour* (Grossman, 2012). Although in these accounts of doing archival research we are in the realm of the imaginary, and ideas about knowledge, dust is a very real and material phenomenon for an archival researcher. All the objects detailed in the participants' written imaginaries – Bronwyn's sharp pencils as well as Jessica's dust motes – underscore the material nature of archival research as well as the symbolic. Archival work happens in particular places – albeit places that have meaningful, symbolic architecture – and involves working with *things*. Desks, for example, are not only places of safety for reclusive scholars, they are also marked by long years of use, as sense of their age can give rise to awe, similar to Bennett's (2001) 'minor experience' that leads to enchantment, or the sense of wonder in ordinary activities and ordinary things. Diana experiences this at the Bodleian's ancient Elizabethan desks, scarred by centuries of writing on their surfaces (Harkness, 2011). In Reimer's memoir, a whole paragraph is devoted to describing in detail the design and marks of age on the old Victorian desks in the British Museum Reading Room. The age of a desk is further evidence (like dust, and books) of scholarship's longevity, an idea underscored by Professor Rossi in *The Historian*, who reminds Paul that the library carrel dates back to seventh-century monasteries (Kostova, 2005). Each desk, like each scholar who inhabits it, performs a part in ensuring that the ever-evolving wheel of scholarship continues to turn; material evidence of that practice is reassuring for researchers.

Desks and books are *things* that have symbolic and cultural meaning. Wonder is often associated with books in the university imaginary, in particular rare, strange or ancient books held in the archive: Grossman's (2012) codex is one such mystical volume; Kostova's (2005) mysterious vellum tome another. Barnett (2011) asks why it was that illuminated manuscripts were lovingly preserved by medieval scholars in libraries, and wonders if it is because they represented encounters with an *other* or meta reality, which gave the work of preservation special meaning. Books and libraries have also been, for centuries, at the centre of Western ideas about what a university *is*. According to Rolfe (2013), until recently reading a book has been *the* defining activity of an academic, and a book the icon of the Enlightenment university. Yet books and the places in which they are housed, as well as places in which to read them, are coming to be understood differently in the contemporary university, in which budgets for print materials steadily shrink. Dare an academic even be seen doing something so anarchic as reading a book on campus these days? – ask scholars of higher education from Brew (2001) to Barnett (2011). Barnett goes on to suggest that because reading is an activity that is private or interior, it requires its *own space*. Yet space is a dwindling commodity in the contemporary university. PhD students have even less reason than academics to feel secure about claims to their own space, and many now 'hot-desk' as the numbers of doctoral candidates steadily increases, adding to the strain on physical resources. In the open-plan space of the contemporary university, like the library at Bannockburn in Collins' (2006) novel, slow interior activities like reading almost seem to be discouraged.

'Desk as text': doctoral research spaces and PhD work

Books and desks have accrued particular symbolic meaning for researchers, but they are not the only *things* described in accounts of research spaces; other mundane objects remind us of the practical and material work of research and also the ways in which ordinary things can be invested with meaning. Margaret Napier, the PhD student in Grossman's (2012) novel, works in the library surrounded by the tools of her trade: a book weight, magnifying glass, sharp pencils, and her Columbia University student ID card. Identity cards and swipe cards are markers of access to the university (or an archive) in both a literal sense and in political terms, as Jones' (2006) infers in *Mr Pip*. In his written imagining, James Burford (PhD, Education) details objects in an imagined office space, including the swipe card which is representative of his 'ability to inhabit the university', a privilege that gives him pleasure but also leads him to reflect on his privileged status as one of the lucky ones *let in*. As a critical scholar of education, James is conscious of issues of access and equity in higher education, and at the same time he is mindful, as a son of an academic, of his own cultural and social capital (Bourdieu, 1986): complexities of meaning which cluster around the card. The ID card also adds to the representation of the research space as protected, as in accounts of archival work above. A sense of safety or security *enables*, or is even a precondition for, PhD work in the texts I have analysed. Ian Brailsford (PhD, History) wrote of the 'security of a cosy space (my departmental office space)' in which he could do his work (archival work) including activities of 'pulling documents out of boxes and reading, note-taking [and] then lots of writing'. The work all took place within the 'cloistered, quiet' and secure space of his 'small office in the History Department' – a space in which he was entitled to be, as a doctoral student, with a paid stipend. These accounts recall Heidegger (1971) in that *things* preserve elements of dwelling, one of which involves being protected or safeguarded.

The small, removed and safe desk scattered with *things* is a core image of the PhD in the cultural imaginary. James Burford writes:

> When I think of the PhD I think of someone working away, high up in a concrete building. They are sitting in an office in front of a computer. They are alone, and focussed . . . The objects I think of are abandoned coffee mugs, stationary, dust, piles of photocopied paper, library books and cans of tuna.

What does this collection of things represent? A life, a body undertaking sustained activity, too focused on work to eat properly, or to clean up, which leads to the detritus of abandoned things. James' description of this space does not fully resemble his actual work space, although he is high up in a concrete building, as his real office has windows. 'But my view is rather lovely, green trees for miles (this doesn't really register in my imagining of the PhD, there is no outside in the picture in my head)'. The interiority of research work, in particular writing, contributes to the symbolic value of particular elements of the work space: the desk and objects utilised by PhD researchers. In Chapter 1, we saw how Isabel shut out the distractions of the outside world while she worked, and how meaningful the room, light and objects inside were for her idea of research. An image Isabel included with her written imaginary to reinforce the idea of focused, interior *work* was of a woman seated at a desk in front of a large computer screen, files piled about her. Although computers do not yet seem to hold the same associations and symbolic value for PhDs as a book or manuscript, they *are* included in twenty-first-century imaginaries of PhD spaces, like those of James and Isabel, and convey something about the nature of contemporary doctoral work. In particular, they are associated with writing and foster that idea of focused activity in an interior space that James and Isabel convey. Computers are also taken-for-granted objects, extensions (as are Bronwyn Lloyd's pencils and notebooks) of the doctoral body and brain in an era of advanced technology.

Yet computers also function as a conduit *out* of the confined interior space by connecting the researcher to other research, via publications online, and to other researchers in a research community. In this way, they represent an idea of research and the university specific to the early twenty-first century (Brew, 2001). In 2003, Robyn Barnacle predicted that the advent of the internet would radically change the very nature of the doctorate; in particular, she identifies a shift in the spatial ordering of doctoral research, with fewer people working in individual offices; a realignment in social dimensions, or how researchers relate to each other; and challenges to traditional forms of knowledge transfer, as access to research communities and other researchers *outside* of one's own institution are opened up. Peters (2003) also predicts (in the same volume) the impact of the internet and suggests that the binary of near and far will be undermined. The idea of a research community beyond the confines of a single university campus (Barnacle, 2003) is what Standaert (2014) refers to with his metaphor of the *network* as an image for the twenty-first-century university, replacing the pillars of the modern university. Both Standaert and Barnacle are signalling a major epistemic shift with the advent of the internet, which has implications for universities and for doctoral research, not least of which is a challenge to ideas of access. Along similar lines, more recently, Peters (2015) identifies the emergence of a 'techno-epistemological epoch' which is changing ways of *being* for a student, academic or university. There are gestures toward these shifts in the contemporary doctoral imaginary, as in James' account, in which the computer brings together the two ideas of the university (as tower and network): his imagined room, high up and away, is accessible only by swipe card, yet is nonetheless *connected*.

Objects, including the university ID card or computer, that appear in representations of PhD spaces can also convey and construct the relationship between the inside and outside of the research space. The lamp creates the light's penumbra for Isabel to dwell and work in, and encloses her in that designated time and the activity of writing. The window in James' written text is a distraction, allowing the real world to intrude, which he absents from his idea of a research space, yet which creeps back in. Other symbolic imagery also has this function. In her imaginary, J. T. (PhD student, Education) reflects on the relationship between the inside and outside of the research space and uses the familiar metaphor of the remote and enclosed ivory tower to represent her fear that doing a PhD would mean not be involved with community in a way that she values – a concern James, who is an activist in the LGBT community, also expressed. There is a movement throughout J. T.'s written text between establishing and questioning binaries: of working alone and working with a community, of being in industry or academia, of reading and writing or doing hands-on fieldwork. The spaces she describes reflect this interaction, which is sometimes figured as two things held in balance, sometimes as a tension:

> The energy of spaces is so important to me. The introverted/extroverted binary that I envisioned plays into the activities in certain spaces. I envisioned mornings alone at home or in a quiet office. This would be in a bit of a sedentary way – reading, writing, thinking (those introverted things). Then I imagined spending afternoons with people – more active, attending facilitating seminars or workshops or meetings. Even outdoors. More social and interactive (extroverted).

The first kind of imagined space she then details further: 'There is an office space I imagine for myself, the centre of my thinking. There is natural light and plants. There are paintings and images on the walls, little scraps of paper with notes on them . . . reminders, quotes, references'. The phrase 'the centre of my thinking' is evocative: does it lie at the centre of her idea of research, or is it where her *thought* is centred, an image for her own mind? This imagined interior space bears some resemblance to Isabel's writing space at home, which came to stand *for* her idea of doctoral research.

However, J. T. sent another piece in which she interprets or reads her actual office space, entitled 'My desk as text: a window interpretation into my life, today' (inspired, she tells me, by Harold Riggins' (1994) *Fieldwork in the living room: an autoethnographic essay*). In 'My desk as text' J. T. interprets the collection of objects on and around her desk (a computer, piles of books, dust, water), reading them as evidence of her life, the life of a researcher, at that time and place. A collage accompanies this written text in which she juxtaposes images of things – as if on a desk – which represents her PhD: putting 'unlikely images together in unexpected ways as a way to develop new understanding (produce new knowledge?)' and 'as a creative, sometimes confusing and sometimes beautiful, and potentially disruptive undertaking.' Her actual space and the collage are full of the unexpected and disruptive in ways that the imagined space is not. The collage includes bottles of beer (representing sociability and industrial production), Post-it notes, lamps (the 'traditional lightbulb/idea metaphor'), an image of a dry desert, a peeled apple, a house lit from within ('stability and inner warmth') and a book. The book, J. T. writes, is:

> an old green book... like the classics or the classical knowledge that underlies the institution... There is both comfort in the old books, but also a warning about who wrote them and for what reason and the impact that these books had and continue to have on structuring society.

The mixed reaction to the book – as a source of comfort and as a warning – epitomises J. T.'s critical engagement with higher education and the PhD, in which she positions herself simultaneously inside and outside. It is her hope that doctoral 'training carves out a particular space for both deeper contemplation as well as social change and critique, and being creative with groups of people'. While deeper contemplation, as represented by her imagined workspace, is valued, it is perhaps the idea of social change and critique that is more meaningful for J. T.. Hopefully, the doctorate enables *both*: 'so I position myself in academia as well as amongst the communities I have worked with'.

The PhD dwelling-place

A political motivation underpins J. T.'s positioning inside/outside academia, like the ideas of researcher positionality included at the end of Chapter 2, but other participants wrote of different motivations or impetuses for a similar positioning. Mercedes (PhD, Art History) deliberately sought out spaces *outside* the university to write during her PhD. She requested that we meet for the follow-up interview in a large hotel lobby in San Francisco – as it turned out this was significant. She began to work in hotel lobbies while in graduate school at the University of Chicago, a campus dominated by modernist concrete structures, which did not offer spaces that she felt comfortable working in. However, the unsuitability of the space had less to do with design than *social* elements. Mercedes is drawn to a particular type of place: public, busy and bustling but not too noisy, familiar and open, and where she can be herself, as she put it. The hotel lobbies enabled her to be alone and anonymous, but also surrounded by human noise and activity. When she moved during the PhD for research – to Chicago, San Francisco, Berlin, Denmark – finding these places and establishing a routine of working in them became very important to her. Mercedes' choice of space seemed *suited* to a sense of self-in-relation-to-others, also signified through factors such as her supervisory relationship (which functioned well yet was not integral to her idea of graduate research) and her internet-based community of fellow researchers, who met virtually and regularly. These elements contribute to an impression of a mobile, independent and self-contained researcher who is nonetheless connected to other researchers. It is an idea which is fairly long-standing, evidenced in travelling scholarships or sabbaticals offered by colonial universities as a way of retaining academic imperial networks (Pietsch, 2013), and which is currently reimagined. In the twenty-first century, academics are increasingly mobile, or nomadic, according to Morley (2012), an idea now underpinned by the highly individualistic ethos of neoliberal global entrepreneurialism 'at the heart' of the contemporary university. According to this reading, the kind of space in which Mercedes chose to work is suited to the contemporary nomadic, global figure of the researcher, who is not housed in a secure and cosy office, but out in the world, alone yet among others, and content to be so.

Mercedes' account of space demonstrates that an identity, or idea of self, is related *to* the spatial in doctoral imaginaries. In Retana's (1998) poem, the Chicano graduate student shifts between feeling confident and feeling out of place as he walks through the campus amid stone buildings and tree-lined avenues. In Lillian's *petit recit*, the distant office signified her social isolation from the other members of the laboratory group, her research status as marginal to the project's aims, and her own keenly felt loneliness.

Another participant, Luke Smythe (PhD, Art History), wrote about his idea of PhD research in which the emergent researcher-self is figured *spatially*. The PhD described by Luke constructs an imagined research space that is nurturing of thought. Before he began the PhD, Luke had an idea of what it would entail, that it would involve 'the kind of thinking, reading and writing I was already doing . . . but with certain institutional benefits and pressures conferred and brought to bear'. He began his doctorate in art history after having conducted research in a private capacity (for artists and galleries) as well as in an institutional context (for his masters' degree), and he saw the institutional contribution (like J. T.) as potentially both 'empowering' *and* 'restrictive'. Specifically, he describes the 'structured ways of doing things' in universities, which had potential to conflict with 'the organic processes of the mind'. Similar to J. T., Luke establishes an interplay (that is for the most part productive) between a series of paired terms: private and institutional, organic and structured, personal and worldly, and empowering and restrictive.

It recalls the dialectic Bachelard (1994) identifies in the poetics of space, between immense and miniature, attic and cellar, light and dark.

The personal idea of the PhD for Luke (ranged alongside the organic, empowering and private) is then explicated in more detail as a 'process of creating a kind of intellectual, experiential "dwelling"'.

> I thought of my dissertation as a kind of intellectual dwelling that I would build or weave together over time, using whatever experiential tools and resources I felt would be useful along the way. Experience would not only provide the tools for this building process, but would itself be the substance from which this dwelling would be made. To write a PhD would be to draw together and articulate different kinds and fragments of experience which would, in some important but hard to fathom way, allow me to more richly inhabit the world.

The dissertation as dwelling is made from materials from experience, gathered 'over time' and 'along the way'. Luke elaborates on these experiences suggesting that the activities of writing and research, and the places where research takes place form a lived layer that contributes to the imagined dwelling:

> I imagined sitting at a desk, whether in a library, an office or at home, reading, writing and thinking. Armchairs, at home, in libraries or in cafés, also cropped up. These environments would form a kind of physical substrate from which my experiential dwelling would emerge. As for how this dwelling might itself be envisaged, I had no concrete imagery. I simply projected an experience of growing satisfaction accruing from the ongoing process of my research. I might describe this satisfaction as 'existential,' since it bears in very general ways on the texture and tenor of my experience in the world.

Luke evokes Heidegger (1971) in drawing together dwelling, thinking and being. He combines *work* (the activities of writing and research) with dwelling, and despite utilising binaries that distance 'institutional' from 'private' work, in the image of his dwelling they satisfyingly combine.

There is no single concrete image for the space that Luke imagines and describes, although he uses verbs of making, building and weaving, and describes a substrate (a subsoil or material on which an organism grows), so it is possible to picture or imagine a dwelling built of natural materials. This is in keeping with Luke's account of the 'organic processes of the mind': 'I can't really describe my dwelling in terms of definite metaphorical imagery. Experientially, though, it boils down to a sense of very deep-rooted satisfaction stemming from my work on the project (so maybe there's a tree metaphor here).' Due to the language (of organic processes) and images (of a substrate, tree, and roots) that Luke uses, I *do* see a structure, although this is not Luke's image: a house made of twigs and branches, like those constructed of willow by artist Patrick Dougherty. There are echoes in Luke's text of Bachelard's (1994/1958) account of images of the hut and the nest, which he describes as simple images of 'felicitous space'. According to Bachelard, a space becomes beloved when we are able to *dream* in it. Once we have lived in a place that is safe, protected, and conducive to repose, elements that foster this state are tucked away as images, to furnish our future imaginaries of felicitous spaces. In this way, memories and the imagination work together, and the many dwelling places we have known in our lives mingle. The state of dreaming or repose that makes a place beloved is not solely to do with rest and sleep; rather, Bachelard sees daydreaming as something akin to *thought*. At times he refers to this state of repose, thinking and daydreaming as simply *inhabiting*.

Bachelard (1994/1958) considers the nest an image for a primal or oneiric image of a home, a simple house that we dream of inhabiting *or* of returning to. In the nest, Bachelard finds the capacity for the dwelling and its inhabitant to be isomorphic or *like* in form. He refers to Jules Michelet's account of bird architecture, of nests constructed by the bird's body. Through the ministrations of the bird, pushing and moulding the nest from the inside, the nest takes shape, so that the dwelling becomes the bird's 'very person'; it is both its form and its 'effort' (Michelet, *L'Oiseau*, 1858, in Bachelard, 1994). If we were, writes Bachelard, to construct dwelling places the way Michelet describes the nest, we would each have a 'personal house' that is 'padded' to our measure. The dwelling Luke describes is likewise an experiential and intellectual space that Luke has constructed in *doing* the PhD, padded to his measure and produced by his effort. It is, to borrow from Bachelard, inscribed in him via 'organic' habits that arise from his experience of doing PhD research, which has provided the substance *and* tools for the building process.

Luke's dwelling is a way of being, a self that emerges out of doing a PhD, and is *satisfied*. The outcome enables Luke to 'more richly inhabit the world':

> Happily, I can say that I was able to realise a satisfying version of my imagined experiential dwelling. I thought about a topic intensively, used it to engage issues I find important, interesting and helpful in negotiating the world, and eventually developed ideas and stories about the world that continue to make my life more enjoyable.

As he takes the experiential dwelling forward into the rest of his life, bringing with him a sense of 'deep-rooted satisfaction stemming from [his] work on the project' and infusing his experience and negotiation of the world with it, Luke registers a profound change in himself. The dwelling now seems less like a nest, which gets left behind once the purpose for which it is built has been achieved, and more like a shell built and worn by snails. Like the bird, the shell of a snail grows *with and around* its body, its shape determined by the being within, yet in this case it is not abandoned, nor is it finished. The shell provides us with images, Bachelard (1994) writes, for emerging; Luke's dwelling has something of this quality.

The dwelling places in which we have daydreamed are, according to Bachelard (1994/1958) reconfigured into new daydreams, or imaginaries, which stay with us even as we go out in the into the world. In a sense, this enables a *return* to the place in which we were sheltered and nurtured when we first came into being. For Bachelard, this is the home, our first home, which comes to stand for 'being-well' or the wellbeing associated with being born and cared for (Bachelard, 1994/1958). The written accounts of PhD research spaces by participants have lead me to wonder if there is *for some* an intellectual equivalent, a space in the (imagined) university in which new academics feel themselves to come into being, which have the associations of home, of nourishment, safety and protection, and which enable daydreaming, repose and thought that is 'being-well'. The safe spaces in the archive evoke this idea, as does Isabel's account of her office space. Perhaps certain spaces of doctoral research, remembered and imagined, provide a dwelling place for PhDs which stays with them, as it has for Luke, and enables them to 'more richly inhabit the world'. For although Luke's dwelling could be seen as precarious, made of insubstantial materials, it nonetheless fosters what Bachelard (1994/1958) terms daydreams of security, like Bradley's (1999) archive, or the offices of Ian or James, which nurture individual subjectivities.

Luke's image offers an important counterpoint to the more instrumental imaginaries of the PhD, such as those which are constructed within a neoliberal frame of discourse, by conveying a sense of satisfaction with research *and in the self* as an outcome. After all, this is one of the traditional aims of a higher education; since the nineteenth century, universities have aimed to foster not only new knowledge, but a realisation of self and identity – *within the built environment* (Newman, 1871; Rothblatt, 2006; Joyce, 2010; Ossa-Richardson, 2014). At the same time, the kind of self and dwelling place that Luke achieves is not realisable for all doctoral students. For some, dwelling, security and nourishment in academia remain a hoped-for but unrealised idea – and the attainment of a stable and singular identity post-PhD is *not* the outcome. Lillian, for instance, wrote not only of her distance from the lab in the scattered office, but also of an unsettled home life during the PhD, and a disillusionment with academia since. She describes being unable to settle outside the lab, away from family and friends, as she moved from flat to flat, seeking both a home and social groups to belong to. In one house, she recalls, she slept out the back in a 'makeshift extra room on the deck' that was tiny, could not fit her desk, and did not have solid substantial walls. The precariousness of Lillian's research status and her isolation permeated her office and home, which did not foster daydreams of security.

The image of Luke's nourishing dwelling space also raises other issues. As Plumwood (2008) reminds, individual love for a place is often established via a disassociation with what she terms shadow places. Her concern is that the influence of Heidegger is taking 'place critique' in a particular direction by emphasising a singular, set-apart space, or 'One True dwelling place' that obscures the problematics of both ecological issues and north/south relations. Despite the potential for speaking back to a utilitarian discourse (as Luke does), the elevation of the 'seat of self' can also recall exclusionary traditions of higher education, according to Plumwood (2008). Privileging a place of self-identity is, she argues, to make invisible (or push into the shadows) the places of the other. This is what Retana (1998) grapples with in his poem – how can he *be* satisfied with his place, having 'made it', while conscious of the fortress that keeps others like him, the 'us' of the final line, out?

The 'seat of self' idea *also* retains, according to Plumwood (2008), the old dualism of mind privileged over body, as the idealised space is identified with an elevated consciousness while what is denied, or glossed over, are the material elements, including economic support, necessary for its attainment. In *Magpie Hall*, Rosemary's attic, where she writes in the old Victorian family mansion, is built on land that was once under the ownership of Maori, the indigenous people of Aotearoa NZ. As Rosemary struggles with her thesis-writing inside, outside the Maori workers struggle to make a living farming the land now owned by Rosemary's family; it is *their* labour which enables the house and farm, and by extension Rosemary's research, to keep on functioning. Cultural practices may evoke idealistic dimensions of space in conceptualising the university, but they *also* pay heed to its exclusionary nature. As we saw in Collins' (2006) novel, the university space is defined by its borders, which represent both expansion *and* exclusion. Likewise, in Retana's (1998) poem, the PhD student-speaker self-consciously walks around a cement worker, who is also Chicano, and who makes the pavement on which the idly strolling students walk.

Concluding remarks
Future imaginings

> For research is the creating of fictions which we then attempt to live.
> (Brew, 2001: 185)

Ideas give way slowly, according to Dewey (1910), for they are not abstractions but deeply ingrained predispositions and attitudes. Long-held ideas linger and mingle, sometimes awkwardly, with the new. Perhaps the imaginary is a repository, a space to hold ideas that are deeply ingrained? The sustained analysis of the cultural imaginary of the PhD that this book has undertaken highlights the presence of Enlightenment ideas in the twenty-first-century PhD imaginary, suggesting that old ideas of the nature and purpose of the Doctor of Philosophy *are* deeply held and ingrained. In the Introduction, I asked if the PhD could be seen as representative of the modern research university (Clark, 2006) in the cultural imagination. Academics sometimes reflect on what might be at the heart of the university, what ideas there are of its *raison d'être* (Derrida, 1994; Readings, 1996; Rothblatt, 2012) and this book has considered what some of those *reasons for being* a university might be in relation to ideas and imaginaries of the PhD. Certainly, as we have seen, there is a looking back tendency in cultural practices and a discursive strain that upholds and extends values attached to reason and knowledge, valorises university libraries and archives, and celebrates PhD researchers as heroes of knowledge. There are fewer attempts in the cultural imaginary to engage with the contemporary entrepreneurial idea of the PhD, which suggests that while it may dominate in some discursive domains, it does not *speak to* broader society in a meaningful way – it has yet to lodge in hearts and minds.

There are also of course tensions that arise from looking back. In this book I have identified a worrying away at the idea of the Enlightenment PhD that includes reflecting on its limitations and contradictions. This is the kind of double-sided engagement that Flint and Peim (2012) argue is currently occurring in educational research more broadly, as we reflect on Western educational traditions and their place in the future. As I have outlined, the lingering traces of a pre-modern or pre-Enlightenment idea of knowledge and the university are also at play in the cultural imaginary. In these traces we find a celebration of mystery and the unknowable, and an engagement with troublesome tropes of madness, loss and desire, things that undermine the Enlightenment ideal, shake up epistemic certainty. These elements are more than a nostalgic reminder of what once was; rather, they have the potential to disrupt, to provoke unease. While the resurfacing of the folk and fantastic, for example, infers something of value, an idea which has a deep hold in the social imaginary of the kind that Taylor (2004) identifies and which bubbles up in contemporary representation, what it could offer now and in the future as a way of resistance to current norms is a lesson we can reflect on. One of the responsibilities of the university is, according to Derrida (2004), to keep alive traditions, or the memory of them, at the same time as fostering openings beyond the traditional for imagined futures.

The presence of diverse or even contradictory ideas about what constitutes the PhD is, I believe, encouraging. To counter the paucity of research-as-the-engine-of-the-economy rhetoric (Brew (2001) terms this the drudgery of commodified knowledge), we need to engage with complex ideas about research and knowledge, including ideas about arcane knowledge sometimes associated with the PhD in cultural practices. If we do this we have a hope of countering the simplistic utilitarian discourse which narrows this highest degree to being *for* jobs, economies, and individual status and mobility. Further, the intersection of different discourses may give rise to productive tensions between old ideas of the university and its purpose, and new ideas, which could lead to openings for further possibilities. This continual engagement with inherited ideas of the PhD, together with the discursive tensions that erupt in representations of it, as examined here, illustrate that while tradition and the ways of the past are of immense value, nothing is so fixed or stable that it is unable to be picked apart, or to change. Tensions – the problematics of the PhD – opens the way for other ideas and new possibilities (Barnett, 2016). As Barnett (2013) argues of the university, we need a *proliferation* of ideas of the PhD, so that we can consider how things might be other, better, than they are.

A premise of this book is that the imagination, and an explicit engagement with works of the imagination, might show us a way to play. By treating popular culture, novels about PhD research, student accounts and research literature as data to analyse, and therefore gain understanding of how the PhD (and by extension the university) is conceptualised, this book underscores the importance *of* the imaginary in contemporary higher education scholarship. Recently Barnett (2013, 2016) has argued for taking account of the university imaginary and utilising the imagination in future planning for the university – all of which I agree with – yet what he terms the social imaginary (also drawing on Taylor (2004)) is lightly interrogated. What *this* book does is place something like that social imaginary, which I have termed the cultural imaginary of the PhD, at the centre of the analysis. This enables reflection on what ideas are encountered by the broader public about the PhD – on television screens, in films, in the pages of a book or newspaper or advertisements. As Barnett (2016) reminds, what is understood *out there* has implications for what happens *in here*, the world of the university, research and scholarship; it effects individuals' decisions about where to go to do a PhD, what to study, how to conduct themselves, how to *be*. Paying attention to the cultural imaginary through the analysis of fictional texts, as well as those produced by or within the institution, also reveals a disruptive strain in the current imaginary. Fiction, as others have argued (Gough, 1998; Gulson and Parkes, 2010) has a tendency to problematize, denaturalise and deconstruct discursive norms, and it has a tendency to signal epistemic ruptures (Burke, 1953; Belsey, 1980; Bakhtin, 1981; Hutcheon, 1999), so has immense potential for critical scholarship of higher education.

One issue that has arisen in the writing of this book is to do with ways in which the cultural imaginary of the PhD perpetuates the idea that higher education in general, and the PhD in particular, is (still) exclusive of certain social groups. Retana's (1998) turn-of-the-century poem confronts this idea: as a Chicano graduate student at a Texan university, the speaker wonders if he is the *only one* – a 'lone star' – despite the ideals of equal opportunity and educational advancement based on merit. The poem highlights a key issue: that access to the institution, such as through targeted admission schemes, scholarships and the like is not the same as access to the forms of knowledge, values and assumptions of higher education that the PhD might be seen to represent. The speaker in Renata's poem tells this tale: he is inside the university, yet stands outside the traditional knowledge structures of it; he cannot find a supervisor who will fit with his ways of thinking. Have things changed since that time? More recently Gale and Hodge (2014) have highlighted that inclusion involves *more* than the counting of bodies; rather, it is to do with taking seriously ways of including other knowledges, other epistemologies and ontologies in higher education, which will truly mean its transformation. The cultural imaginary of the PhD as traced here is so strongly tied to a Western idea/ideal of knowledge, and of the individual self, that *other* ways of knowing, being and thinking are not yet, not really, included.

Yet, I wonder if we can detect a willingness to engage with other knowledges in the cultural imaginary of the PhD? The regularity with which imagined researchers come up against finds that threaten to destabilise their accepted systems of knowledge, and the recurrence of mystery, folk tale and wonder, for instance, tells us that there is an openness or perhaps even a desire to think outside or beyond the modern Western episteme. I wonder what ideas about the PhD shaped by non-Western educational traditions (Singh, 2009) could now and in the future inform our conceptualisations of the degree? While the cultural practices I have analysed occasionally gesture to other knowledges, it is usually in terms of the limits of what is known or knowable in the frame of Western Enlightenment systems of knowledge, as considered in Chapter 1, yet there is potential for further openings, looking toward other cultural and educational traditions.

As I was putting the final touches on this book, I was at a conference in which around 100 academics were gathered to talk about the measured university: on the first day the conversations kept coming back to what I think of as *hard ideas*. Hard ideas are those we worry away at, and which, because they are difficult, tend to be left to philosophers to try to define. In the early twentieth century, novelist Iris Murdoch wrote of *the hard idea of thought* – a phrase which has worried away at me since my own PhD. Hard ideas are difficult to measure, unlike numbers of research outputs, numbers of doctoral students, and so on. Hard ideas are what academics are apparently encouraged *not* to include in learning outcomes for courses these days, terms like 'to know' and 'understand', because they are difficult to assess. In the late twentieth century, Readings (1996) argued that it should be 'Thought' (rather than the empty 'excellence') that the university placed at its core. Thought: difficult, hard to measure and surely, surely, a core *of* the university. If a traditional responsibility of universities is to remember tradition, to be a repository, according to Derrida (2004), the other is to foster *thinking*. That morning at the conference I heard other hard ideas, including knowledge, being, self, soul, mystery, thinking, imagining, labour, desire, love, the infinite, beauty, God, conscience and – the university. I was struck both by a sense of relief (from the language of measurement and audit) and also by how seldom, nowadays, outside of the odd conference, I hear these ideas in and about the university. Yet I *do* come across them, all the time, in the cultural imaginary of the PhD. In the literary and popular imagination, these are the very ideas that define the university and the PhD: they are its troublesome heart, that make it worth worrying away at.

References

Aikin, S. H. (1986) 'Women and the Question of Canonicity,' *College English* 48 (3): 288–299.

Aitchison, C., Kamler, B. and Lee, A. (2010) *Publishing Pedagogies for the Doctorate and Beyond*, Abingdon: Routledge.

Akerlind, G. (2008) 'An Academic Perspective on Research and Being a Researcher: An Integration of the Literature,' *Studies in Higher Education* 33 (1): 17–31.

Althusser, L. (1994/1971) 'Ideology and Ideological State Apparatuses,' in Storey, J. (ed.) *Cultural Theory and Popular Culture: A Reader*, New York: Harvester (151–162).

Anderson, A. (2009) 'The Way We Talk about the Way We Teach Now,' *Profession*: 19–27.

Apple, M. W. (2006) 'Rhetoric and Reality in Critical Educational Studies in the United States,' *British Journal of Sociology of Education* 27: 125–144.

Archer, L. (2008) 'The New Neoliberal Subject? Young/er Academics' Constructions of Professional Identity,' *Journal of Education Policy* 23 (3): 265–285.

Bachelard, G. (1994/1958) *The Poetics of Space*, Massachusetts: Beacon Press.

Bakhtin, M. (1981) *The Dialogic Imagination: Four Essays*, Texas: University of Texas Press.

Bansel, P. (2011) 'Becoming Academic: A Reflection on Doctoral Candidacy,' *Studies in Higher Education* 36 (5): 543–556.

Barnacle, R. (2003) 'Virtual Research Practices and Phenomenologies of the Internet,' in Edwards, R. and Usher, R. (eds) *Space, Curriculum and Learning*, Connecticut: Information Age Publishing (173–188).

Barnacle, R. (2005) 'Research Education Ontologies: Exploring Doctoral Becoming,' *Higher Education Research and Development* 24 (2): 179–188.

—— and Dall'Alba, G. (2011) 'Research Degrees as Professional Education?', *Studies in Higher Education* 36 (4): 459–470.

—— and Dall'Alba, G. (2013) 'Beyond Skills: Embodying Writerly Practices through the Doctorate,' *Studies in Higher Education* 39 (7): 1139–1149.

Barnett, R. (1994) *The Limits of Competence: Knowledge, Higher Education and Society*, Buckingham: SRHE/Open University Press.

—— (2000) *Realising the University in an Age of Supercomplexity*, Maidenhead: McGraw-Hill/SRHE.

—— (2011) *Being a University*, Abingdon: Routledge.

—— (ed.) (2012) *The Future University: Ideas and Possibilities*, Abingdon: Routledge.

—— (2013) *Imagining the University*, Abingdon: Routledge.

—— (2016) *Understanding the University*, Abingdon: Routledge.

Barthes, R. (1977) *Image/Music/Text*, London: Fontana Press.

Belsey, C. (1980) *Critical Practice*, London and New York: Methuen.

—— (1994) *Desire: Love Stories in Western Culture*, Oxford: Blackwell.

Bennett, J. (2001) *The Enchantment of Modern Life: Attachment, Crossings and Ethics*, Princeton: Princeton University Press.

Bones (2005-) United States: Fox Media.

Booth, A. (2002) 'Neo-Victorian Self-help, or Cider House Rules,' *American Literary History* 14 (2): 284–310.

Bosanquet, A., Winchester-Seeto, T. and Rowe, A. (2012) 'Social Inclusion, Graduate Attributes and Higher Education Rurriculum,' *Journal of Academic Language & Learning* 6 (2), 73–87.

Boud, D. and Lee, A. (2009) *Changing Practices of Doctoral Education*, London: Routledge.

Bourdieu, P. (1986) 'The Forms of Capital,' in Richardson, J. (ed.) *Handbook of Theory of Research for the Sociology of Education*, New York: Greenwood Press (241–258).

Bradley, H. (1999) 'Seductions of the Archive: Voices Lost and Found,' *History of the Human Sciences* 12 (2): 107–122.

Brew, A. (2001) *The Nature of Research: Inquiry in Academic Contexts*, London: Routledge.

Burford, J. (2015) 'Queerying the Affective Politics of Doctoral Education: Toward Complex Visions of Agency and Affect,' *Higher Education Research and Development* 34 (4): 776–787.

Burke, K. (1953) *Counter-Statement*, California: University of California Press.

Byatt, A. S. (1990) *Possession: A Romance*, London: Chatto & Windus.

—— (1996) *Babel Tower*, London: Chatto & Windus.

—— (2000) *The Biographer's Tale*, London: Chatto & Windus.

—— (2002) *A Whistling Woman*, London: Chatto & Windus.

Carter, S., Kelly, F. and Brailsford, I. (2012) *Structuring your Research Thesis*, London: Palgrave Macmillan.

Cham J. (1997-) *Piled Higher and Deeper: A Grad Student Comic Strip*. Available at http://www.phdcomics.com/comics.php.
Cixous, H. (1993) 'Sorties,' in Cixous, H. and Clement, C., *The Newly Born Woman*, Minneapolis: University of Minnesota Press.
Clark, W. (2006) *Academic Charisma and the Origins of the Research University*, Chicago: University of Chicago Press.
Clegg, S. (2008) 'Academic Identities under Threat?', *British Educational Research Journal 34* (3): 329–345.
Collini, S. (2008) *Common Reading: Critics, Historians, Public*, Oxford, Oxford University Press.
—— (2012) *What are Universities For?* London: Penguin.
Collins, M. (2006) *The Secret Life of E. Robert Pendleton*, London: Weidenfeld & Nicolson.
Connell, R. (2007) *Southern Theory: The Global Dynamics of Knowledge in Social Science*, Australia: Allen & Unwin.
Cronon, W. (1983) *Changes in the Land: Indians, Colonists and the Ecology of New England*, Canada: HarperCollins.
Cruikshank, J. (1998) *The Social Life of Stories: Narrative and Knowledge in the Yukon Territory*, Lincoln, New England: University of Nebraska Press.
Culler, J. (1997) *Literary Theory: A Very Short Introduction*, Oxford: Oxford University Press.
Cumming, J. (2007) 'Representing the Complexity, Diversity and Particularity of the Doctoral Enterprise in Australia,' PhD Thesis, Centre for Educational Development and Academic Methods, The Australian National University, Canberra.
—— (2009a) 'Representing Doctoral Practice in the Laboratory Sciences,' in Boud, D. and Lee, A. (eds) *Changing Practices of Doctoral Education*, Abingdon: Routledge (113–125).
—— (2009b) 'The Doctoral Experience in Science: Challenging the Current Orthodoxy,' *British Educational Research Journal 35* (6): 877–890.
Daston, L. J. and Park, K. (2001) *Wonders and the Order of Nature*, New York: Zone Books.
Davies, B. (2005) 'The (Im)possibility of Intellectual Work in Neoliberal Regimes,' *Discourse: Studies in the Cultural Politics of Education 24* (1): 1–114.
Dawson, P. (2010) 'The Death of a Beautiful Woman' [extract], *Southerly 70* (2): 143–157.
Derrida, J. (1982/1972) 'White Mythology: Metaphor in the Text of Philosophy,' in *Margins of Philosophy*, Chicago: Chicago University Press (207–272).
—— (1995) *Mal d'Archive: Une Impression Freudienne*, Paris: Editions Galilée.
—— (2004/1990) 'Punctuations: The Time of a Thesis,' in *Eyes of the University: Right to Philosophy 2*, Stanford: Stanford University Press (113–128).
—— (2004/1983) 'The Principle of Reason: The University in the Eyes of its Pupils,' in *Eyes of the University: Right to Philosophy 2*, Stanford: Stanford University Press (129–155).

Dunn, M. (2012) 'Direct from the Kiln; Laird and Lange's Clay Library,' *EyeContact.*

Dunleavy, P. (2003) *Authoring a PhD: How to Plan, Draft, Write and Finish a Dissertation or Thesis*, London: Palgrave Macmillan.

Earwacker, J. and Becker, K. (2002) *The Scene of the Crime: A Guide to the Landscapes of British Detective Fiction*, Great Britain: Aurum Press.

Eik-Nes, N. L. (2008) 'Front Stage and Back Stage Writing: Using Logs to Rehearse and Develop a Disciplinary Role,' *Nordic Journal of English Studies* 7 (3): 181–198.

Flint, K. J. and Peim, N. (2012) *Rethinking the Education Improvement Agenda: A Critical Philosophical Approach*, London: Continuum.

Folsom, E. (2007) 'Database as Genre: The Epic Transformation of Archives,' *PMLA 122* (5): 1571–1579.

Foucault, M. (1977) *Discipline and Punish: The Birth of the Prison*, London: Penguin.

—— (1991/1971) 'Nietzsche, Genealogy, History,' in Rabinow, P. (ed.) *The Foucault Reader: An Introduction to Foucault's Thought*, London: Penguin, 76–100.

—— (1994/1970) *The Order of Things: An Archaeology of the Human Sciences*, London: Vintage.

Forster, E. M. (1992/1919) *Howard's End*, London: Penguin.

Gale, T. and Hodge, S. (2014) 'Just Imaginary: Delimiting Social Inclusion in Higher Education,' *British Journal of Sociology of Education 35* (5): 688–709.

Gill, J. (2009) 'Practical Knowledge,' *Times Higher Educational Supplement*, 26 February.

Giroux, H. (1992) *Border Crossings: Cultural Workers and the Politics of Education*, New York: Routledge.

Golde, C. (2000) 'Should I Stay or Should I Go? Student Descriptions of the Doctoral Attrition Process,' *Review of Higher Education, 23* (2) 119–127.

—— (2005). 'The Role of the Department and Discipline in Doctoral Student Attrition: Lessons from Four Departments,' *The Journal of Higher Education* 76 (6): 669–700.

Goodman, A. (2006) *Intuition*, London: Atlantic Books.

—— (2010) *The Cookbook Collector*, London: Atlantic Books.

Gonzalez, C. R. (2008) 'A Dialogue with Literary Theory: A. S. Byatt's *The Biographer's Tale*,' *English Studies* 89 (4): 447–460.

Gough, N. (1998) 'Reflections and Diffractions: Function of Fiction in Curriculum Inquiry,' in Pinar, W.F. (ed.) *Curriculum: Toward New Identities*, New York: Garland Publishing (94–127).

—— (2004) 'Read Intertextually, Write an Essay, Make a Rhizome: Performing Narrative Experiments in Educational Inquiry,' in Piper, H. and Stronach, I (eds) *Educational Research: Difference and Diversity*, England: Ashgate (15–176).

—— (2010) 'The Truth is Not Out There: Becoming "Undetective" in Social and Educational Enquiry,' in Walker, M. and Thomson, P. (eds) *The Routledge Doctoral Supervisor's Companion*, London: Routledge (231–246).

Gowers, R. (2009) *The Twisted Heart: A Literary Murder Mystery and a Tale of Modern Love*, Edinburgh: Canongate Books.
Grant, B. (1997) 'Disciplining Students: The Construction of Student Subjectivities,' *British Journal of Sociology of Education* 18 (1): 101–114.
—— (2005) 'Fighting for Space in Supervision: Fantasies, Fairytales and Fallacies,' *International Journal of Qualitative Studies in Education* 18 (3): 337–354.
—— (2008) 'Agonistic Struggle: Master-slave Dialogues in Humanities Supervision,' *Arts and Humanities in Higher Education: An International Journal of Theory, Research and Practice* 7 (1): 9–27.
Green, B. (2005) 'Unfinished Business: Subjectivity and Supervision,' *Higher Education Research and Development* 24 (2): 151–163.
—— (2009) 'Challenging Perspectives, Changing Practices: Doctoral Education in Transition,' in Boud, D. and Lee, A. (eds) *Changing Practices of Doctoral Education*, Abingdon: Routledge (239–248).
Gregory, M. (2007) 'Real Teaching and Real Learning vs Narrative Myths about Education,' *Arts and Humanities in Higher Education: An International Journal of Theory, Research and Practice* 6 (1): 7–27.
Grieg, D. and Wilson, W. (2011) *The Strange Undoing of Prudencia Hart*, National Theatre of Scotland.
Grossman, L. (2012) *Codex*, New York: Mariner Books.
Gulson, K. and Symes, C. (2007) 'Knowing One's Place: Educational Theory, Policy and the Spatial Turn,' in Gulson, K. and Symes, C. (eds) *Spatial Theories of Education: Policy and Geography Matters*, Abingdon: Routledge.
—— and Parkes, R. (2010) 'Bringing Theory to Doctoral Research,' in Walker M. and Thomson P. (eds) *The Routledge Doctoral Student's Companion*, Abingdon: Routledge (76–84).
Gumprecht, B. (2007) 'The Campus as Public Space in the American College Town,' *Journal of Historical Geography* 33, 72–103.
Gunn, K. (2012) *The Big Music*, London: Faber and Faber.
Hall, S. (1996) 'Who Needs "Identity"?' in Hall, S. and du Gay, P. (eds) *Questions of Cultural Identity*, London: Sage (1–17).
Hardy, T. (1985/1895) *Jude the Obscure*, London: Penguin.
Harkness, D. (2011) *A Discovery of Witches*, London: Headline.
Hayles, N. K. (1990) *Chaos Bound: Orderly Disorder in Literature and Science*, Ithaca: Cornell University Press.
Heidegger, M. (1971/1954) 'Building Dwelling Thinking,' in *Poetry, Language, Thought*, New York: Harper and Row (145–61).
Hopwood, N. (2014) 'The Rhythms of Pedagogy: An Ethnographic Study of Parenting Education Practices,' *Studies in Continuing Education* 36 (2): 115–131.
—— and Paulson, J. (2010) 'The Body in Doctoral Education: Towards a Research Agenda,' Second International Doctoral Education Research Network Conference, Kuala Lumpur, April 19–23.
Hutcheon, L. (1999) *A Poetics of Postmodernism: History, Theory, Fiction*, New York and London: Routledge.
Jacobs, L. (2009) *The Bird Catcher*, New York: St Martin's Press.

James, H. (1985/1881) *The Portrait of a Lady*, New York: Viking.
—— (1995/1898) *The Turn of the Screw*, Boston: Bedford Books of St. Martin's Press.
Johnson, L., Lee, A. and Green, B. (2000) 'The PhD and the Autonomous Self: Gender, Rationality and Postgraduate Pedagogy,' *Studies in Higher Education* 25 (2): 135–47.
Jones, L. (2006) *Mr Pip*, Wellington: Victoria University Press.
Joyce, P. (2010) 'What is the Social in Social history?' *Past and Present 205*: 175–210.
Kearns, H. (2008) 'Innovation in PhD Completion: The Hardy Shall Succeed (and be Happy!),' *Higher Education Research and Development 27* (2): 151–163.
Keen, S. (2001) *Romances of the Archive in Contemporary British Fiction*, Toronto: University of Toronto Press.
Kelly, F. (2009) 'Supervision Satirised: Fictional Narratives of Student-Supervisor Relationships,' *Arts and Humanities in Higher Education 8* (3): 368–384.
—— (2012) 'Seekers after Truth? Images of Postgraduate Research and Researchers in the Twenty-first Century,' *Discourse: Studies in the Cultural Politics of Education 33* (4): 517–528.
—— (2013) 'And so Betwixt Them Both: Taking Insights from Literary Analysis into Higher Education Research,' *Higher Education Research and Development 32* (1): 70–82.
—— (2016) 'The Time of the PhD: Doctoral Research in Neo-Victorian Fiction,' *Neo-Victorian Studies Journal* (forthcoming).
—— and Brailsford, I. (2012) 'From Student to Academic: Doctoral Candidates' Transition to Understanding Academic Work,' Quality in Postgraduate Research Conference, Adelaide, April 16–20.
King, R. (2009) *Magpie Hall*, Auckland: Random House.
Knights, B. (2005) 'Intelligence and Interrogation: The Identity of the English Student,' *Arts and Humanities in Higher Education: An International Journal of Theory, Research and Practice 4* (1): 33–52.
Kostova, E. (2005) *The Historian*, London: Little, Brown and Company.
Kristeva, J. (1995) *The Kristeva Reader*, edited by Toril Moi, Oxford: Blackwell.
Laird, T. (2013) *Chupacabra Candelabra*. Freedom Farmers Exhibition, Auckland: Auckland City Art
Lather, P. (2006) 'Paradigm Proliferation as a Good Thing to Think With: Teaching Qualitative Research as a Wild Profusion,' *Qualitative Studies in Education 19* (1): 35–57.
Lea, M. and Stierer, B. (2011) 'Changing Academic Identities in Changing Academic Workplaces: Learning from Academics' Everyday Professional Writing Practices,' *Teaching in Higher Education 16* (6): 605–616.
Lee, A. and Green, B. (2009) 'Supervision as Metaphor,' *Studies in Higher Education 34* (6): 615–630.
Lefebvre, H. (1991/1974) *The Production of Space*, Oxford: Blackwell.
Lenz Taguchi, H. (2013) '"Becoming Molecular Girl": Transforming Subjectivities in Collaborative Doctoral Research Studies as Micro-politics in the Academy,' *International Journal of Qualitative Studies in Education 26* (9): 1101–1116.

Llamas, J. M. C. (2006) 'Technologies of Disciplinary Power in Action: The Norm of the "Good Student",' *Higher Education 52*: 665–686.

Lloyd, B. (2011) *The Second Location*, Auckland: Titus Books.

Lodge, D. (1965) *Changing Places: A Tale of Two Campuses*, London: Secker & Warburg.

—— (1984) *Small World: An Academic Romance*, London: Secker & Warburg.

Lovitts, B. (2007) *Making the Implicit Explicit: Creating Performance Expectations for the Dissertation*, Sterling, VA: Stylus Publishing.

Lurie, A. (1984) *Foreign Affairs*, New York: Random House.

Lyotard, J. F. (1993/1979) *The Postmodern Condition: A Report on Knowledge*, Minneapolis: University of Minnesota Press.

MacLure, M. (2003) *Discourse in Educational and Social Research*, Buckingham: Open University Press.

—— (2013) 'The Wonder of Data,' *Cultural Studies ↔ Critical Methodologies 13* (4): 227–233.

Mahoney, S., Park, Z. and Smyth, R. (2013) *Moving On Up: What Young People Earn after their Tertiary Education*, Wellington, NZ: New Zealand Government.

Maltman, T. (2012) *Little Wolves*, New York: Soho Press.

Mamet, D. (1992) *Oleanna*, London: Methuen/Royal Court Theatre.

Manathunga, C. (2005) 'Early Warning Signs in Postgraduate Research Education: A Different Approach to Ensuring Timely Completions,' *Teaching in Higher Education 10* (2): 219–233.

——, Cornforth, S., Crocket, K., Court, M. and Claiborne, L. B. (2013) 'Irruptions of Space and Bodies in Doctoral Supervision,' *Knowledge Cultures 1* (5): 60–80.

Manathunga, C. (2014) *Intercultural Postgraduate Supervision: Reimagining Time, Place and Knowledge*, Abingdon: Routledge.

McAlpine, L. and Lucas, L. (2011) 'Different Places, Different Specialisms: Similar Questions of Doctoral Identities under Construction,' *Teaching in Higher Education 16* (6): 695–706.

McDermott, M. and Daspit, T. (2005) 'Vampires on Campus: Reflections on (Un)death, Transformation, and Blood Knowledges in *The Addiction*,' in Edgerton, S., Holm, G., Daspit, T. and Farber, P. (eds) *Imagining the Academy: Higher Education and Popular Culture*, New York: RoutledgeFalmer (231–246).

McGann, J. (1991) *The Textual Condition*, Princeton, NJ: Princeton University Press.

—— (2007) 'Database, Interface and Archival Fever,' *PMLA 122* (5): 1588–1592.

McWilliam, E. (2009) 'Doctoral Education in Risky Times,' in Boud, D. and Lee, A. (eds) *Changing Practices of Doctoral Education*, Abingdon: Routledge (189–199).

Mewburn, I. (2011) 'Troubling Talk: Assembling the PhD Candidate,' *Studies in Continuing Education 33* (3): 321–332.

Meyer, J. H. F., Shanahan, M. P. and Laugksch, R. C. (2005) 'Students' Conceptions of Research: A Qualitative and Quantitative Analysis,' *Scandinavian Journal of Educational Research 49* (3): 225–244.

Mieville, C. (2009) *The City and the City*, London: PanMacmillan.
Morley, L. (2012) 'Imagining the University of the Future,' in Barnett, R. (ed.) *The Future University: Ideas and Possibilities*, New York: Routledge (26–35).
Morrow, J. (2009) *The Philosopher's Apprentice*, London: Weidenfield & Nicolson.
Moss, S. (2012) *Night Waking*, London: Granta.
Murphy, P. (2015) 'Discovery and Delivery: Time Schemas and the Bureaucratic University,' in Gibbs, P. et al. (eds) *Universities in the Flux of Time: An Exploration of Time and Temporality in University Life*, London: Routledge (137–154).
Newman, J. H. (1996/1871) *The Idea of the University*, edited by F. M. Turner, New Haven and London: Yale University Press.
Niffenegger, A. (2009) *Her Fearful Symmetry*, London: Jonathan Cape.
Nussbaum, M. (1997) *Cultivating Humanity: A Classical Defence of Reform in Liberal Education*, Cambridge, MA: Harvard University Press.
O'Callahan, J. (2013) 'Degrees Ranked by Earning Potential,' *Dominion Post*, Wellington, NZ. Available at: http://www.stuff.co.nz/national/education/8205505/Degrees-ranked-by-earning-potential.
Ossa-Richardson, A. (2014) 'The Idea of a University and its Concrete Form', in Temple, P. (ed.) *The Physical University: Contours of Space and Place in Higher Education*, Abingdon: Routledge (131–158)
Owler, K. (2010) 'A "Problem" to be Managed? Completing a PhD in the Arts and Humanities,' *Arts and Humanities in Higher Education* 9 (3): 289–304.
Park, C. (2007) *Redefining the Doctorate*, York: The Higher Education Academy. Available at: http://www.grad.ac.uk/downloads/documents/Reports/HEA/RedefiningTheDoctorate.pdf
Parker, J. (2009) 'Academics' Virtual Identities,' *Teaching in Higher Education* 14 (2): 221–224.
Pearson, M. (2005) 'Framing Research on Doctoral Education in Australia in a Global Context,' *Higher Education Research and Development* 24 (2): 119–134.
Peters, M. (2003) 'Geographies of Resistance in Critical Pedagogic Practices,' in Edwards, R. and Usher, R. (eds) *Spatiality, Curriculum and Learning*, Buckingham: Open University Press (189–200).
—— (2015) 'The University in the Epoch of Digital Reason,' in Gibbs, P. et al. (eds) *Universities in the Flux of Time: An Exploration of Time and Temporality in University Life*, London: Routledge (9–31).
Petersen, E. B. (2011) 'Staying or Going? Australian Early Career Researchers' Narratives of Academic Work, Exit Options and Coping Strategies,' *Australian Universities' Review* 53 (2): 34–52.
Pietsch, T. (2015) *Empire of Scholars: Universities, Networks and the British Academic World 1850–1939*, London: Palgrave.
Plumwood, V. (2008) 'Shadow Places and the Politics of Dwelling,' *Australian Humanities Review* 44, 139–150.
Readings, B. (1996) *The University in Ruins*, Cambridge, MA: Harvard University Press.
Reimer, A. (1998) *Sandstone Gothic*, St. Leonards, N.S.W: Allen & Unwin.

Retana, N. (1998) 'The Hopwood Doctorate,' *Qualitative Studies in Education 11* (1), 3–4.
Robinson, K. S. (1997) *Antarctica*, Hammersmith: HarperCollins.
Rolfe, G. (2013) *The University in Dissent: Scholarship in the Corporate University*, London: Routledge.
Rossen, J. (1993) *The University in Modern Fiction: When Power is Academic*, New York: St Martin's Press.
Rothblatt, S. (1997) *The Modern University and its Discontents: The Fate of Newman's Legacies in Britain and America*, Cambridge: Cambridge University Press.
—— (2006) 'The University as Utopia,' in Neave, G., Blucket, K. and Nybom, T. (eds) *The European Research University: An Historical Parenthesis?* Palgrave Macmillan (29–49).
—— (2012) 'The Future Isn't Waiting,' in Barnett, R. (ed.) *The Future University: Ideas and Possibilities,* New York: Routledge (15–25).
Russell, W. and Gilbert, L. (1983) *Educating Rita*, UK: Columbia Pictures.
Russo, R. (2009) *That Old Cape Magic,* London: Chatto & Windus.
Saltmarsh, S. (2009) 'Haunting Concepts in Social Research,' *Discourse: Studies in the Cultural Politics of Education, 30* (4), 539–546.
—— (2011) 'Economic Subjectivities in Higher Education: Self, Policy and Practice in the Knowledge Economy,' *Cultural Studies Review 17* (2), 115–139.
Schatzki, T. (2002) *The Site of the Social: A Philosophical Account of the Constitution of Social Life and Change,* Pennsylvania: Pennsylvania State University Press.
Schmitt, F. F. and Lahroodi, R. (2008) 'The Epistemic Value of Curiosity,' in *Educational Theory 58* (2), 125–148.
Segre, M. (2015) *Higher Education and the Growth of Knowledge: A Historical Outline of Aims and Tensions,* New York: Routledge.
Shore, C. and Wright, S. (1999) 'Audit Culture and Anthropology: Neo-liberalism in British Higher Education,' *The Journal of the Royal Anthropological Institute* 5 (4), 557–575.
—— (2010) 'Beyond the Multiversity: Neoliberalism and the Rise of the Schizophrenic University,' *Social Anthropology 18* (1): 15–29.
Siegel, J. (1981) 'Academic Work: The View from Cornell,' *Diacritics 11* (1): 68–83.
Singh, M. (2009) 'Using Chinese Knowledge in Internationalising Research Education: Jacques Ranciere, an Ignorant Supervisor and Doctoral Students from China,' *Globalisation, Societies and Education 7* (2): 185–201.
Smiles, S. (1859) *Self-help: With Illustrations of Conduct and Perseverance.* EBSCO Publishing.
Smith, Z. (2005) *On Beauty,* London: Penguin.
Somerville, M. (2010) 'A Place Pedagogy for Global Contemporaneity,' *Educational Philosophy and Theory 42* (3): 326–344.
Sousanis, N. (2015) *Unflattening,* Cambridge, MA: Harvard University Press.
Standaert, N. (2014) 'Towards a Networked University,' in Barnett, R. (ed.) *The Future University: Ideas and Possibilities,* New York: Routledge (87–100).

Steedman, C. (2001) *Dust*, Manchester: Manchester University Press.
Sturm, S. and Turner, S. (2011) 'Built Pedagogy: The University of Auckland Business School as Crystal Palace,' *Interstices 12*, 23–34.
Tartt, D. (1993) *The Secret History*, London: Penguin.
Taylor, C. (2004) *Modern Social Imaginaries*, Durham: Duke University Press.
Temple, P. (2014) *The Physical University: Contours of Space and Place in Higher Education*, London: Routledge.
Tennant, M. (2005) 'Doctoring the Knowledge Worker,' *Studies in Continuing Education 26* (3): 431–441.
Thomson, P. and Walker, M. (2010) 'Doctoral Education in Context: The Changing Nature of the Doctorate and Doctoral Students,' in Walker, M. and Thomson, P. (eds) *The Routledge Doctoral Supervisor's Companion: Supporting Effective Research in Education and the Social Sciences*, Abingdon: Routledge (9–26).
—— and Kamler, B. (2013) *Writing for Peer Reviewed Journals: Strategies for Getting Published*, London: Routledge.
Verschueren, P. (2015) 'Webs of Analysis. A Network Analysis of Change in an Academic Field: The Case of the Physical Sciences in France 1944–1968,' *Science, Technologies and Material Culture in the History of Education: History of Education Society Annual Conference*. Liverpool: Liverpool Hope University: November.
Walker, G. E., Golde, C. M., Jones, L., Conklin Bueschel, A. and Hutchings, P. (2008) *The Formation of Scholars: Rethinking Doctoral Education for the Twenty-First Century*, Stanford: The Carnegie Foundation for the Advancement of Teaching/Jossey-Bass.
Waugh, E. (2009/1943) *Brideshead Revisited*, London: Penguin.
Were, V. (2013) 'Rainbow Serpents and Other Awakenings,' *Art News New Zealand* (Summer).
Whyte, W. (2015) *Redbrick: A Social and Architectural History of Britain's Civic Universities*, Oxford Scholarship Online: Oxford University Press. Available at: www.oxfordscholarship.com
Willig, L. (2005) *The Secret History of the Pink Carnation*, Sydney: Bantam Press.
Wilson, A. N. (2005) *A Jealous Ghost*, London: Hutchinson.
Wisker, G. (2007) *The Postgraduate Research Handbook*, London: Palgrave Macmillan.
—— (2012) *The Good Supervisor*, London: Palgrave Macmillan.
Womack, K. (2002) *Post-war Academic Fiction: Satire, Ethics, Community*, Basingstoke: Palgrave.
Woolf, V. (1989/1929) *A Room of One's Own*, London: Penguin.
Yeatman, A. (1998) 'Making Research Relationships Accountable: Graduate Student Logs,' in Lee, A. and Green, B. (eds) *Postgraduate Studies / Postgraduate Pedagogy*, Sydney, Australia: University of Technology (21–30).
Ylijoki, O.H. (2008) 'A Clash of Academic Cultures: The Case of Dr. X,' in Välimaa J. and Ylijoki, O.-H. (eds) *Cultural Perspectives on Higher Education*, New York: Springer (75–88).

Youdell, D. (2004) 'Engineering School Markets, Constituting Schools and Subjectivating Students: The Bureaucratic, Institutional and Classroom Dimensions of Educational Triage,' *Journal of Educational Policy 19* (4): 407–431.

Zembylas, M. and Michaelides, P. (2004) 'The Sound of Silence in Pedagogy,' *Educational Theory 54* (2): 193–210.

Zhang, Z. (2014) '"Let's Go for the Chicken Drum": The Everyday Production of Social Space in a Chinese University,' in Temple, P. (ed.) *The Physical University: Contours of Space and Place in Higher Education*, Abingdon: Routledge, (182–202).

Zgaga, P. (2009) 'Higher education and citizenship: 'the full range of purposes',' *European Educational Research Journal 8* (2): 175–188.

Index

academics *see* researchers
access 119
The Addiction (film) 63
advertisements 49–51, 55–57
Aikin, Susan Hardy 103
alliances 85, 89
Althusser, Louis 52
Antarctica (Robinson) 31, 32, 85, 87
anxiety 38
Archer, L. 64
archives 17, 100–107, 117
Arts and Humanities Research Council 61
associationism 95, 98
audit culture 45, 48, 49, 64
Australia 7, 53, 56
authenticity 100, 102

Babel Tower (Byatt) 94
Bachelard, Gaston 1, 35, 37, 38, 93, 101, 113–115
Bakhtin, Mikhail 7
Bansel, Peter 49, 52, 58
Barnacle, Robyn 38, 62, 109
Barnett, Ron: idea of the university 2, 3, 9; institutionalised work 34; libraries 107; loss of mystery 14, 25; new knowledge paradigms 19, 20; social imaginary 118–119; wonder 30
Belsey, C. 18
Bennett, Jane 10, 11, 28–29, 31, 106
The Big Bang Theory (TV show) 88–89
The Big Music (Gunn) 37
binaries 37, 46–47, 90, 110
The Biographer's Tale (Byatt) 16, 70–72, 76, 77
The Bird Catcher (Jacobs) 78
Blanchot, Maurice 39–40
Bodleian Library 100, 103, 104, 105, 106, 107
body 44, 79, 81–83, 90
'body of knowledge' metaphor 46, 47
Bones (TV show) 16, 53–54, 55, 56, 57, 58, 85
books 25, 26–27, 33, 100–101, 106–107, 111
Booth, A. 47–48
border-crossers 61–62
Bradley, Harriet 100, 104, 115
Brew, Angela 14, 15, 92, 102, 105–106, 107, 117, 118

Brideshead Revisited (Waugh) 93
British Library 102, 103, 105
British Museum 100, 103, 105–106, 107
Burgess, Bob 54
Butler, Judith 52
Byatt, Antonia Susan 19, 75, 76, 78, 79; bodily actions 90; doctoral pedagogy 70–72; libraries and archives 103, 105–106; power and gender in supervision 81–83; research as discovery 16, 18; research groups 84; university towers 94

campus design 92–93, 94–96
career choices 51–52
Carlyle, Thomas 32–33, 36
Cham, Jorge 39, 55, 70, 72–75, 83, 85, 90
chance 14, 17, 27
change 10, 12
charisma 14, 20, 31, 44–45, 78–79, 85
China 35, 92, 93
Chupacabra Candelabra (Laird) 26–27, 28, 40n1
The City and the City (Mieville) 29–30, 31
Cixous, Hélène 46, 77
Clark, William 2, 31, 39, 44–45, 48, 87; collections 22–23, 25, 27; writing 32
Codex (Grossman) 106
collaboration 80–81
Collaborative Doctoral Partnership scheme 61
collection, research as 21–27
Collini, S. 47
Collins, Michael 96–99, 100, 105, 107, 116
competition 18, 64, 88
computers 109, 110
constellations 85
consumerism 92
The Cookbook Collector (Goodman) 26
Cornell University 93, 96–97
corporate universities 9
creativity 15, 39, 45
Cruikshank, J. 12
Culler, Jonathan 46
cultural imaginary 10, 11, 14, 117–118, 119–120; mystery and wonder 32; objects 108; spaces of doctoral research 91, 92, 94, 96, 105; supervision 79; *see also* social imaginary
cultural practices 11, 30, 91, 116, 117
culture 7
Cumming, Jim 66, 84, 87, 88
curiosity 15, 18, 31

Dall'Alba, G. 38, 62
Daspit, T. 63
Daston, L. J. 23, 25, 27, 28, 31
Davies, B. 59, 63
Dawson, P. 67
degrees 5
Deleuze, G. 62
Derrida, Jacques 3–4, 20, 21, 33, 97, 100, 105, 118, 120
desks 106–107, 108–109, 110–111
detective fiction 16–21
Dewey, John 117
dialogue 68
Dickens, Charles 47
discourse 6–7, 10, 43, 44, 65–66
discovery 13, 15, 16–21
dissertations 22, 113
domestic labour 37
doubled gaze 59
Dougherty, Patrick 114
Dust (Steedman) 106
dwelling 113–116
dyad, supervision as a 68, 69–77

earnings 51–52
economic development 48–49
ecosocial pedagogy 68–69, 85
Educating Rita (film) 77–78, 93
educational research 8, 18–19, 117–118
efficiency 9, 34
Eik-Nes, N. L. 65–66
Eliot, George 18, 47
embodiment 44, 83
Enlightenment 2–3, 5, 23, 44, 117; 'body of knowledge' metaphor 46, 47; discourse 43; hero of knowledge figure 42, 45; knowledge 25, 27, 28, 120; legacy of the 62; light and truth 15; mind/body split 79; researcher-self 20; wonder 28
entrepreneurial universities 2, 9

eros 79
ethics 49, 64–65

fiction 8, 32, 90, 119; about writing 37–39; libraries and archives 102–103, 104, 105–106; power and gender in supervision 78, 79–83; private pedagogy 70–77; research as discovery 16–21; university campuses 93, 95–99
fields of identification 69, 84
flexibility 42, 45, 63
Flint, K. J. 7, 117
folk tales 23, 24, 120
Folsom, Ed 102
forensic research 56–57
Forster, E. M. 78
Foucault, Michel 2, 28, 52
fragmented academics 59–60

Gale, T. 119
Galileo 1, 15, 61
gender 77–83, 88
Germany 2, 3, 7, 22, 23
Gill, J. 54
global knowledge economy 5–6, 9
global researchers 50–51
Goffman, Erving 65
Gonzalez, C. R. 71
Goodman, Allegra 26, 84, 85
Gough, Noel 8, 18–19
Gowers, Rebecca 16, 18, 104
Grant, B. 11, 52, 71, 72, 74, 77
Great Britain 2, 7, 47, 61, 75
Green, B. 66, 68–69, 73, 85
Greig, David 23
Grimm, Jacob and Wilhelm 23
Grossman, L. 41, 49, 106, 107, 108
group pedagogy 68, 84–90
Guattari, F. 62
Gulson, K. 8, 92
Gunn, Kirsty 37

Hall, S. 20
hard ideas 120
Hardy, Thomas 93
Harkness, D. 104, 105
haunting 21
Hayles, N. K. 19

Heidegger, Martin 38, 39–40, 93, 108, 113, 116
The Historian (Kostova) 16, 17–18, 20, 21, 32, 83, 99, 104, 107
history 8
Hodge, S. 119
home 115
Hopwood, N. 66
Howard's End (Forster) 78

ID cards 108, 110
identity 34, 41, 44, 54; alternative academic identities 58–66; place and 116; realisation of 115; spatial doctoral imaginaries 112; *see also* self
images 1–2, 4, 5, 11
imaginaries 4–5, 8–10, 11–12, 14, 117; discourse and representation 6; dwelling places 115; spatial 112; writing 34, 39; *see also* cultural imaginary; social imaginary
imagination 39, 118–119
inclusion 119
independence 42, 44, 45, 47
individualism 51–52, 64, 112
intellectual capital 58
interdisciplinarity 7–8, 50, 89
intertextuality 7, 18–19, 46, 75
Intuition (Goodman) 84

Jacobs, Laura 78
James, Henry 75, 76
A Jealous Ghost (Wilson) 75–77
Johnson, L. 3, 20, 46, 47, 48
Jones, Lloyd 102–103, 105, 108
Joyce, Patrick 90, 95
Joyce, Steven 51, 59
Jude the Obscure (Hardy) 93

Kamler, B. 34, 39
KE *see* knowledge economy
King, Rachael 16, 18, 37, 79–80
Knights, B. 76
knowledge: body of 46, 47; contribution to 5, 13–14, 42; drudgery of commodified 118; economic development 48; Enlightenment 25, 27, 28, 120; 'hero of' 3, 4, 39, 42, 44, 45, 117; hidden

repositories of 99; intellectual capital 58; for its own sake 2–3, 14; light and truth 105; objective 18, 19; originality 15; specialist 45; useful 54; as way of being and becoming 62–63; Western idea of 119; writing 32, 38, 39–40

knowledge economy (KE) 5–6, 9, 42, 43, 45, 52, 63

knowledge workers 6, 42, 43, 45

Kostova, Elizabeth 24, 27, 67, 90, 105; books 107; power and gender in supervision 83; research as discovery 16, 17–18, 20, 21; spaces of doctoral research 91

laboratory settings 84–85, 86–87, 88–89, 90
labour, research as 34, 35–36, 106
Lahroodi, R. 31
Laird, Tessa 26–27, 28
language 6, 28, 44
Leavis, F. R. 78
Lee, A. 58
Lefebvre, H. 93, 100–101, 102
Lenz Taguchi, H. 62–63
libraries 25, 100–107, 117
light 15, 105
literary culture 7, 14, 16; *see also* fiction
literary studies 8
Llamas, J. M. C. 52
Lodge, David 19, 75, 76
loneliness 86–87, 112
Lovitts, B. 15
Lurie, A. 75
Lyotard, J. F. 11

MacLure, M. 6, 8, 27, 28, 87
Magpie Hall (King) 16, 37–39, 79–80, 116
Mahoney, S. 52
Mamet, David 78
managerialism 9
Manathunga, C. 68, 69, 71, 75, 83
marginalisation 86–87
markets 44–45
materiality 66, 90, 102
McDermott, M. 63
McWilliam, Erica 58, 83

metaphorical locations 69
method 17, 18
Mewburn, I. 65–66
Meyer, J. H. F. 15
Michelet, Jules 114
Mieville, China 29–30
mind/body split 44, 79, 82–83, 90, 116
mobile academics 112
monastic scholarship 34–35, 102
Morley, L. 112
Morrow, James 78
Moss, Sarah 39
Mr Pip (Jones) 102–103, 108
Murdoch, Iris 120
Murphy, P. 13, 15
mystery 14–15, 18, 25, 30, 32, 118, 120
myths 93

National Art Library 101, 103–104, 105
national progress 48
neoliberalism 8–9, 21, 42–43, 51, 115; doubled gaze 59; flexibility in neoliberal discourse 45, 63; individualism 64, 112
nests 114–115
New Zealand 7, 33–34, 45, 49–51, 86, 116
Newman, Cardinal John Henry 3, 94–95
Night Waking (Moss) 39
non-completion 43, 55
North American campuses 95–99
nostalgia 93
Nussbaum, M. 49

objects 107–111
obsessive researchers 57–58
Oleanna (Mamet) 78
On Beauty (Smith) 78
oral exams 52–54
originality 5, 13–14, 15
Ossa-Richardson, A. 92, 94
'other' PhDs 55–58
Owler, K. 39–40
Oxbridge tutorials 68
Oxford University 21, 93–95, 103, 104

Park, K. 23, 25, 27, 28, 31
Parker, Jan 78–79, 83
Parkes, R. 8
Paulson, J. 66

Index

pedagogy 4, 67–90; group 84–90; power and gender in supervision 77–83; private 68, 69–77
Peim, N. 7, 117
perfectionism 39
Performance Based Research Fund (PBRF) 33–34
performativity 33
person v.s. product 42
personal development 51
Peters, M. 109
Petersen, E. B. 64
The Philosopher's Apprentice (Morrow) 78
Piled Higher and Deeper (PhD Comics) (Cham) 39, 72–75, 88
Piled Higher and Deeper: The PhD Movie 85
Plato 62
Plumwood, V. 116
poetics 1–2, 113
policies 14
popular culture 7, 10, 30–31, 118; gender in supervision 77–78; mystery 14; PhD scholars 42, 43; research as discovery 16
Possession: A Romance (Byatt) 16, 18, 70, 75, 76, 79, 103, 105–106
postmodernist discourses 44
postmodernity 19, 63
power 74–75, 80, 81
practices 9, 10, 66; cultural 11, 30, 91, 116, 117
procrastination 39, 75
professional researchers 54
profile of doctoral researcher 45–49

rationality 14, 45, 92; *see also* reason
Reading Room (Laird) 26
Readings, B. 120
realism 51, 55
reality 6
reason 20, 42, 44, 45, 62, 105, 117; *see also* rationality
Reimer, Andrew 69, 75, 78, 91, 94, 102–103, 107
repertories 4–5
representation 6–7, 10, 41, 90; cultural 1–2; pedagogy 68; representational space 100–101; universities 93–94

research: archives 100, 101; as collection 21–27; constellations 85; as discovery 15, 16–21; idea of 41–66; interdisciplinary 7–8; mystery 14–15; originality 13–14; spaces of 91–116; wildernesses in 11; wonder 27–32; writing 32–40
research universities 2, 3, 4, 9, 30, 32, 117; *see also* universities
researchers 42, 43, 44–66; alternative academic identities 58–66; as collectors 21–22; fully developed 49–55; mobile 112; 'other' PhDs 55–58; profile of doctoral researcher 45–49; as seekers of truth 20–21
Retana, N. 103, 112, 116, 119
risk 33, 38, 78
rituals 53
Robinson, Kim Stanley 31, 32, 85, 87, 89
Rolfe, G. 107
Rothblatt, S. 3–4, 92, 95–96, 102
Ruskin, John 32
Russo, Richard 80–81

Saltmarsh, S. 21, 59
Sandstone Gothic (Reimer) 69, 75, 103
Schatzki, T. 10, 68, 90
'schizophrenic' universities 59
Schmitt, F. F. 31
science 18, 51, 85, 87, 88–89
The Secret History (Tartt) 76
The Secret Life of E. Robert Pendleton (Collins) 96–99
Segre, M. 61
self 43, 44, 45; in discourse 65–66; dwelling as a way of being 114; realisation of 115; 'seat of' 116; *see also* identity
self-awareness 47
self-development 42, 47, 62, 70–71
Self-help (Smiles) 47–48
self-management 33, 39
Serres, Michel 63
Shakespeare, William 12n1
Shore, C. 9, 59
Siegel, J. 93, 97
Simmons, - 59
skills 6, 42, 45–46, 47, 54, 58–59
slow academics 64
Smiles, Samuel 47–48

Smith, Zadie 78
social context 39
social imaginary 4–5, 9, 11–12, 30, 84, 118–119; *see also* cultural imaginary
social orders 68
socialisation 65–66, 84, 86, 89, 91–92
Somerville, M. 93
Sousanis, N. 62
space 91–116; campus design 92–93, 94–96; dwelling 113–116; imagined research space 112–113; libraries and archives 100–107; non-university spaces 111–112; North American campuses 95–99; work spaces and objects 107–111
Standaert, N. 109
standardisation 5
status 2
Steedman, Carolyn 102, 106
stories 4, 5, 11–12
The Strange Undoing of Prudencia Hart (Greig & Wilson) 23–24, 25, 27, 31
student choice 51–52
students, number of doctoral 42
Sturm, S. 92
subjectivity 4, 44, 52, 59; *see also* identity
supervision 4, 67–90; gender, power and the body 77–83; group pedagogy 68, 84–90; metaphorical locations 69; private pedagogy 68, 69–77
Symes, C. 92

Tartt, Donna 76
Taylor, Charles 4–5, 9, 10, 11–12, 30, 84, 118
technologies of the self 43
Temple, Philip 92
Tennant, M. 47
texts 6, 11
That Old Cape Magic (Russo) 80–81
thesis writing 32–40
'thing-power' 10
Thomson, P. 34, 39, 48, 49
time 5, 34
Trapido, B. 41
'troubles talk' 65–66
truth 15, 16, 18–19, 20–21, 105
The Turn of the Screw (James) 75, 76, 77
Turner, S. 92

tutorials 68
The Twisted Heart: A Literary Murder Mystery and a Tale of Modern Love (Gowers) 16–17, 18, 24

Unflattening (Sousanis) 62
United States 2, 7, 95–96
universities 10, 21, 117; academic identities 60–61; borders 116; campus design 92–93, 94–96; film and literary representations 93–94; idea of the university 2, 3–4, 9, 94; libraries and archives 100–107; North American campuses 95–99; originality 15; purpose of 13; responsibilities of 118; 'schizophrenic' 59; spatial dimensions 91–92; 'thought' at the heart of 120; traditional and modern 44; wonder 30–31; writing as central to 32–33
University of Berlin 2
University of Chicago 111
University of London 103

viva voce 52–54

Walker, M. 48, 49
Waugh, Evelyn 93
Weber, Max 14, 44
Were, V. 26
Western culture 7, 17, 35, 77, 105, 119–120
A Whistling Woman (Byatt) 81–83, 84, 94
Whyte, W. 95
Williams, E. 58
Willig, Lauren 13, 16
Wilson, A. N. 70, 75–77
Wilson, Wils 23
women 36, 37, 77–83, 103
wonder 27–32, 107, 120
Woolf, Virginia 36, 37, 103
work, research as 34, 35–36, 106, 113
writing 4, 23, 32–40

Ylijoki, O. H. 59
Youdell, D. 52

Zhang, Z. 92, 93
Žižek, Slavoj 12n1

Taylor & Francis eBooks

Helping you to choose the right eBooks for your Library

Add Routledge titles to your library's digital collection today. Taylor and Francis ebooks contains over 50,000 titles in the Humanities, Social Sciences, Behavioural Sciences, Built Environment and Law.

Choose from a range of subject packages or create your own!

Benefits for you
- Free MARC records
- COUNTER-compliant usage statistics
- Flexible purchase and pricing options
- All titles DRM-free.

Benefits for your user
- Off-site, anytime access via Athens or referring URL
- Print or copy pages or chapters
- Full content search
- Bookmark, highlight and annotate text
- Access to thousands of pages of quality research at the click of a button.

Free Trials Available
We offer free trials to qualifying academic, corporate and government customers.

eCollections – Choose from over 30 subject eCollections, including:

Archaeology	Language Learning
Architecture	Law
Asian Studies	Literature
Business & Management	Media & Communication
Classical Studies	Middle East Studies
Construction	Music
Creative & Media Arts	Philosophy
Criminology & Criminal Justice	Planning
Economics	Politics
Education	Psychology & Mental Health
Energy	Religion
Engineering	Security
English Language & Linguistics	Social Work
Environment & Sustainability	Sociology
Geography	Sport
Health Studies	Theatre & Performance
History	Tourism, Hospitality & Events

For more information, pricing enquiries or to order a free trial, please contact your local sales team: **www.tandfebooks.com/page/sales**

 The home of Routledge books

www.tandfebooks.com